795

HENDERSON

Peter ~~Stull~~

Bath 8AM Tues. Cori

Eat Out 5AM

Weds BK.

ṬÁHIRIH THE PURE

WITH MARTHA
by Marzieh Gail

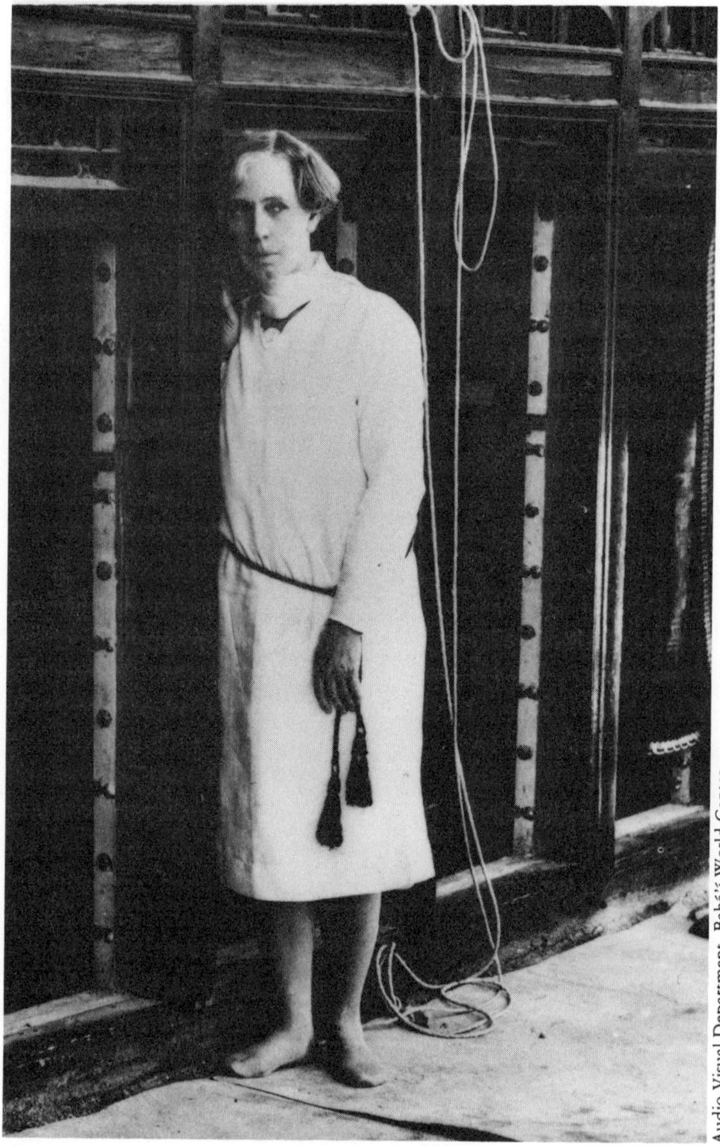

Audio-Visual Department, Bahá'í World Center

MARTHA ROOT
at the House of the Báb, Shíráz, Iran

ṬÁHIRIH THE PURE

BY

MARTHA L. ROOT

Revised Edition
with an introductory essay by
MARZIEH GAIL

KALIMÁT PRESS
LOS ANGELES

Originally published as *Ṭáhirih the Pure: Irán's Greatest Woman*
in 1938 in Karachi by Martha L. Root. This revised edition
has been printed by permission of the
National Spiritual Assembly of the Bahá'ís of Pakistan.

Revised Edition

Manufactured in the United States of America

Library of Congress Cataloging in Publication Data

Root, Martha L
Ṭáhirih the pure.

Originally published in 1938 under title: Ṭáhirih
the pure, Iran's greatest woman.
Includes bibliographical references.
1. Qurrat al-'Ayn, 1817 or 18-1852. 2. Bahaism—
Iran—Biography. I. Title.
BP395.Q87R66 1980 297'.89'0924 [B] 80-39945
ISBN O-933770-14-6

COVER DESIGN: Engraving of the Royal Palace at Iṣfahán, circa 1840.

CONTENTS

"With Martha" by *Marzieh Gail* 1

Introduction 33

Chapter I: Early History of Ṭáhirih's Life 43

Chapter II: Events in Qazvín and Ṭihrán 69

Chapter III: Ṭáhirih's Martyrdom 95

Epilogue 117

Appendix I: Ṭáhirih's Poems 119

Appendix II: Bahá'u'lláh's Tribute to the Báb 132

Appendix III: The World Religion by *Shoghi Effendi* 135

Notes 140

WITH MARTHA

by Marzieh Gail

I WAS ENJOYING a lemon ice in the lobby of the big hotel in Belgrade. I looked out the plate glass window and there, hurrying past, I saw a small, female figure in a dark coat and brown straw hat. Beneath the hat I saw the line of an indomitable jaw, and I saw it was Martha Root, intent upon her tasks. Isolated, purposive, concentrated, she might have been all alone on the planet. I sighed, guiltily.

"It's some job, keeping up with Martha," my diary says. "Stamps fly, and wires are hot."

"Martha's method is straight-from-the-shoulder," I recorded. "She hasn't been with a person three minutes before she's given him a book or picture. This next is an exaggeration. She'll say to him or her: 'How do you do? Here is a picture of 'Abdu'l-Bahá. I love you.' "

A few lines from my diary, jotted down during the more than three weeks when Martha and I and my first husband Howard Carpenter were together, will help to illustrate the incredible, day-by-day services, carried on over a period of virtually twenty years, of this woman whom the Guardian calls "that archetype of Bahá'í teachers," the "star-servant" and "foremost Hand" of the first Bahá'í century.[1] We recall that she came to us exhausted, after achieving results in Prague that she herself wrote were "miraculous." A letter of mine says: "Martha's here—lovelier than ever, and so tired. She'll give eight lectures in six days. . . ."

Vienna: "At the von Rosthorns' for tea. Martha gave them some candied fruit. Their guests also heard of the Cause. . . . Martha's meeting for the Bahá'ís. . . . Called on the Thern sisters and daughter Vida—they met the Master here. . . . [I realized later on that in Vienna and Budapest Martha was actually doing follow-up work for 'Abdu'l-Bahá, Who pioneered here, and looking up people who had been in His presence]. . . . Martha addressed the American Women's Club. . . . Martha lunched with Queen Marie of Rumania and Arch-Duchess Anton, later spoke at the Theosophists'. Here she quoted eminent Theosophists who had told her: 'Theosophy is a philosophy; Bahá'í is a universal religion.' Said we both agree on the principle of development, only not the place. Quoted Mrs. Besant's statement that 'Abdu'l-Bahá was the greatest living man. . . . We had to get Martha through a howling mob to her lecture at the Quakers'. . . . Martha spoke in Hall 38 at the University of Vienna. Von Rosthorn arranged this and served as her chairman. . . . A professor called on Martha, said it was a question whether Gandhi or Swiss scientist Forel was the greater. Martha told him that on her tour of Swiss cities, the editors everywhere said they had heard of the Bahá'í Faith through Dr. Forel. . . . We left Vienna and came to Györ. Mr. Steiner told Martha he has finished translating Esslemont into Hungarian. Martha spoke on world peace, in a hall rented for her by a non-Bahá'í. . . .''

Budapest: ''Called on Rustum Vambéry, son of the famed Orientalist. Called on Professor Nadler, and saw his painting (from life) of 'Abdu'l-Bahá. . . . Martha spoke to a large group at the Women's League for Peace and Freedom. Met tons of people. Interviewed by the press. She gave out many books, as usual. Talked to a packed crowd in Hotel Gellert. . . .''

Belgrade: ''Called on U.S. Minister [Ambassador] John D. Prince, a great linguist. Martha was invited to tea with Prince Paul and Princess Olga. He represents the king, is most popular and influential. A bishop asked us to lunch, but we couldn't go, due to another engagement. Several well-known professors were interested. Martha arranged for the translation of the Serbian Esslemont. Called on Esperantists, very friendly to Martha. Evening with the Anthroposophists. . . . Martha addressed large group at the Esperantists', and many came on to her second lecture at the Women's League. She made me chant at every function, whether I wanted to or not. Secretary at American Legation [Embassy] says our coming has precipitated many a theological discussion there. Martha's university extension lecture, after which she was up till midnight teaching one of the professors. . . . People called all next day. Went to the station to see Martha off. The Esperantists were there in full force, and honoring her—she is one of their best—they brought along a green flag on a cane, to wave."

That afternoon at the station, incidentally, was the last time I ever saw Martha. I knew from experience that as the train pulled out, she would be standing in the corridor, her hand waving up and down, and she saying over and over: "Alláh-u-Abhá. Alláh-u-Abhá."

And so on and on she traveled—not young or strong, not beautiful, not rich, alone, and more than once in terrible danger—on and on, for twenty years. She had begun these journeys in response to 'Abdu'l-Bahá's mandate to America, issued in His Tablets of the Divine Plan. That was 1919. She was the first to arise,[2] and she carried on with her work until, far from home, she stumbled and fell "in her tracks." Died September 29, 1939, in agony after months of physical torment.

That grave of hers, under a rainbow shower tree in Honolulu, is like so many Bahá'í graves that dot the planet—they are tenanted by exiles. I think of Canada's May Bolles

Maxwell, far to the south in Buenos Aires; or of my father Ali-Kuli Khan, born in Káshán, buried in the capital city of the United States; or of Dr. Susan I. Moody, much-loved American, who lies in Ṭihrán among the people she served so long and well. The very geography of their graves expresses their devotion to Bahá'u'lláh.

I USED TO ASK myself why people would do what Martha wished. "When a person says no," was Martha's view, "that's the time to begin persuading him." It took you back to that well-known dialogue in *Henry IV:*

> Glendower: I can call spirits from the vasty deep.
> Hotspur: Why, so can I . . . but will they come when you do call for them?

In Martha's case, yes, they would. They seemed to know they were meant to; they seemed to recognize and respect what she was.

"In each town," I wrote, not without wonder, "she goes to the most important people and they do the rest. You should see people who aren't Bahá'ís translating the books, arranging lectures, being chairmen at this and that function, studying the Teachings . . . and after Martha has been in a place for a while she starts a study class."

Her lectures were clear and plain. If embellished by literary allusions or displays of wit, I recall none of them. One reason may have been that during much of her life she spoke to audiences who were not born to English, and on these the nuances, the things not said, the connotations familiar in England and America would generally be lost. (You would, in such circumstances, push a familiar button, and nothing would happen.)

As for her voice, it has been recorded, humanity will hear it always. It was not unmusical; it was flutey and clear; earnest, emphatic; very fresh and spiritual, and with none of the preacher's pear-shaped tones. Her tempo was slowish, adapted to the translator. Each word was clearly pronounced. Distinguished is the way I would describe her English speech. Absent for years from the United States, she had neither the flatness nor the nasal quality of some American speakers, and she used the broad *a*. Her two other languages were, so far as I remember, Esperanto and some French. She had a good ear: her recording shows that she said the Greatest Name correctly, pronouncing both *l*'s, breathing the *h (Al-láh-ho Ab-há)*.

I heard many of Martha's talks (sometimes, God forgive me, I thought too many: I was a fan of Keith's).[3] Martha usually followed the same general pattern, her travels naturally furnishing much of the content. She would tell of this or that leader whom she had interviewed, and who had given her a tribute to our Faith. I can still hear her saying: ". . . and he said. . . ." And I can still hear her saying "Bahá'í means Light-Bearer." (Well, yes and no. I would say it means "follower of Bahá"; "one who belongs to the Glory of God.")

Take the lecture she gave to the American Women's Club in Vienna. I could not help, as we went along that afternoon, contrasting her world renown with the actual humble circumstances of her daily life. "It is remarkable how Martha endures cold, and insufficient food," my diary says; she traveled steerage, third class, on crowded street cars, lived in poor rooms. Now she was walking ahead, one hand holding up folds of her ankle-length, pale blue satin dress to keep it out of Vienna's winter mud; it was the very dress she had worn for her first audience with Queen Marie. Over it she wore a straight, dark coat, and she had on a brown straw hat—this was early February—with a leather belt around the crown. I worried some, knowing the audience would be worldly, and dressed in big furs and high Russian boots; I wondered how a small, plain, older woman would appeal to them.

She spoke to these women entirely on the Bahá'í Cause. She told them about Ṭáhirih, and how her death as the world's first martyr for women's rights had inspired Marianna Hainisch, mother of a President of Austria, to say: "I shall try to do for the women of Austria what Ṭáhirih gave her life to do for the women of Persia." She reported what the statesmen she had visited had said in tribute to the Bahá'í Faith. She told them how at one time she herself was ashamed to be seen carrying a Bahá'í book; how she left the book in a drug store and the druggist's wife read it and became a Bahá'í. How she, Martha, studied the Faith two years before looking up any Bahá'ís at all.

I need not have worried. At the end, those women flocked around her. And Martha, following her usual custom, presented the club with Dr. Esslemont's book.

Again, there was her talk one winter's night for the Bahá'ís of Vienna. In her usual way, she described the progress of the Faith (and it really was astonishing, when you remember that, at that time, in all of the United States there were perhaps only fifteen hundred Bahá'ís). She told how Fanny Knobloch had shed tears in South Africa, and later on the house where she had wept became a Bahá'í house. How Fanny had started a Bahá'í class there by walking up and down a street and ringing door bells. How Martha herself, traveling third class on a ship, had given a Bahá'í talk, and five hundred attended from the first class, and two hundred from the second. She also gave us, that night, the words of

MARTHA ROOT

the Greatest Holy Leaf, daughter of Bahá'u'lláh, and First Lady of the Faith: Khánum had said that if, after death, she should be found worthy to meet her Father, the first thing she would ask Him would be His help for the Bahá'ís.

Years after, when I was back in Vienna again, Franz Pöllinger told me that some of the believers who heard Martha that night were put to death in the Hitler time.

That night, thirty-three of us signed a letter to the Guardian, and we raised $16 for the House of Worship, then being built at Wilmette.

MOSTLY, MARTHA was alone, but if there were Bahá'ís in a place, she wrote ahead, and they did what they could to prepare for her. I happened to be in Vienna on my way to Persia, where the Guardian had written me to go. My husband, Howard Carpenter, had his M.D. from Stanford University, and we were spending some months in Austria so that he could work at his specialty with the great Viennese ophthalmologists of that day. We had letters of introduction from San Francisco doctors, and met people like the famous Max Pollak, who in after years would make a notable etching of 'Abdu'l-Bahá. Meanwhile we helped the Vienna community when we could, I filling speaking engagements as they developed, Howard teaching a class on *The Dawn-Breakers* for those who knew English.

Meanwhile Martha kept writing ahead, and practicing her usual cross-pollination; she sent us a professor from one of Europe's great universities, who was planning a journey to Ṭihrán. Martha ceaselessly introduced people to one another, shared books and letters, did favors all over the globe, carefully set down names and addresses in an infinite number of poorly classified notebooks.

For Martha never limited her task to the platform. There were the people who came to her. There were her own visits in each town: to newspaper offices (a journalist, she had a high regard for the press), to government and civic leaders, to universities, societies, clubs, whatever—she knocked, and went through the doors that opened. It all meant long, jerky trips on crowded public transport, hanging on any which way and carrying heavy books, being lost in strange cities, having accidents (like the time she fell and broke her glasses), being confused by the noise of foreign tongues, soaked by the rains, chilled by the snows, battered by the winds of all five continents.

As for the professor, in those days, especially in Europe, professors were important. They were not just one of the boys. You looked up to them.

"I hope," said Howard dubiously, "he isn't disappointed by our youthful appearance."

In any case he came, and stayed three days.

AS THE GUARDIAN writes, Martha was also, "on more than one occasion," in "extremely perilous circumstances."[4] The fact that she was not physically brave only increases her stature. Morally, yes. But rumor was that, unlike some Bahá'ís, she did not long for martyrdom. She herself asks of Ṭáhirih in this book: ". . . did she too, need to be trained by the Infinite God to long to give her life . . . ?" (p. 3).

One night in Vienna we three were briefly in some

danger, when we had to pilot Martha through a near riot to her lecture at the Quakers'. I remember the torchlight parade in front of the Opera, the kicking, swerving police horses and trembling police, the thousands upon thousands of people howling in the night. Suddenly the light flashed on a dark face amidst all those light skins and the mob began to snarl, then to hiss and hiss (it still takes me back to Satan's welcome in Milton, when he reaches home after seducing Eve). "She was scared to death," the diary says, "but I knew Howard would get us through."

THERE IN AUSTRIA we found a German pioneer, Franz Pöllinger, a slight, fair man, with eyes like green jewels, but almost sightless. One day in Stuttgart (it was May 23, 1916), Franz had been discussing the question of Truth with a friend. Something made him cry out, "Wahrheit, Wahrheit, über alles!"[5] Because of his cry, the friend's wife gave him the Bahá'í Message. Franz became a believer, and had two Tablets from 'Abdu'l-Bahá, besides letters from the Guardian. Blind or not, he taught himself English, the better to serve, and he earned his living as a masseur. "He works very hard, and only thinks of the Cause," the diary says. As he worked on his clients, he would tell them of the Bahá'í Faith. It was through him that some of Vienna's fine homes were opened to us, and later on to Martha, because his clients, although worldly people in a class-conscious society, were so impressed with Franz's character that they called him a "saint" and an "apostle," and would accept any friend he introduced.

It was Franz who took us, and later Martha, to Exzellenz

Artur von Rosthorn, noted sinologist at the university, former ambassador (and a man to whom Pierre Loti pays tribute in *The Last Days of Peking*). "This lecture he arranged for Martha at the university is the crowning event of his career," said Franz, "and he is supposed to be an atheist."

Franz lived, and held meetings, in a small, medieval room, upstairs in a "Wine and Beer House," on an ancient street, and he had affixed the Bahá'í principles to the street door. Wages being what they were in Vienna that year, we felt guilty to think how much, out of regard for our comfort, he must be spending on extra coal for his ancient stove.

ALTHOUGH I HAVE always taken everything Martha did for granted—she was Martha, that was enough—still I have wondered how she, to outward seeming an unnoticeable, average little woman, with no worldly credentials, ever took it into her head to approach the remote, bejewelled and glamorous Queen Marie of Rumania, daughter of the Duke of Edinburgh, granddaughter of that Victoria who, 'Abdu'l-Bahá affirms, "was superior to all the kings of Europe. . . ."[6]

I have asked myself by what magical coincidence she had brought the Bahá'í Message to Marie in one of the darkest moments of the queen's life.

"It came," Marie has written, "as all great messages come, at an hour of dire grief . . . the seed sank deeply." Again she wrote: "Indeed a great light came to me with the Message of Bahá'u'lláh and 'Abdu'l-Bahá. . . . We pass the Message from mouth to mouth. . . ." And in one of her public tributes she says: "The Bahá'í Teaching brings peace to the soul and hope to the heart. To those in search of assurance the words of the Father are as a fountain in the desert after long wandering.''

Martha had simply, on arriving in Bucharest, sent Her Majesty the Esslemont book, *Bahá'u'lláh and the New Era,* together with a note. Late into the small hours, Marie had read the book, and two days afterward, on January 30, 1926, she granted Martha an audience in the Controceni Palace.[7]

In Vienna, during our stay, the queen received her at Mödling. Martha genuinely, it seemed to me, loved the woman she called ''Her dear Majesty.'' ''I am sure of the queen,'' she once told me—meaning the queen's strong faith. One year, during an audience, Marie pinned a family possession to Martha's dress—a treasured brooch, two wings of gold and silver, set with tiny diamond chips, and joined by a single large pearl. As was her custom, Martha instantly gave the gift away: she sent it to Wilmette to be sold for the Bahá'í Temple, and there it was bought by Willard Hatch, who presented it to the International Bahá'í Archives in the Holy Land.

''MARTHA ALWAYS FEELS her decisions are the Will of God,'' my diary says.

Her career shows that she was an individual who knew her own mind. As with a number of our leading pioneers, I could not visualize her enduring the day-to-day, in-harness participation required by the consultative procedures of Bahá'í Assembly and committee life. When she happened to encounter another equally strong-minded individual, the results were not uninteresting. Rumor had it that on one occasion, in the Hawaiian Islands, Martha and the well-

Audio-Visual Department, Bahá'í World Center

MARTHA ROOT

known Agnes Alexander contemplated some joint teaching venture. Martha drew up a plan of action which she felt was inspired by spiritual guidance; at the same time Agnes also devised a plan which she too believed to be divinely guided. The only trouble was, the two plans were diametrically opposite.

I was once caught in the middle of just such a clash, between Martha and my husband Howard. It was in Belgrade, at the small hotel where we stayed (not the grander one where I had the ice). Howard had been able to persuade Martha into the little hotel, a step up from her usual hospice, but for meals, she would still boil an egg on a tripod in her wash basin, and finish off luxuriously with an apple and a piece of cheese. (This of course gave Howard the opportunity to warn her she might fall a victim to acute alcoholism, from her spirit lamp.)

On this day, Howard was upstairs in our room, sick. Martha was a couple of floors below. Martha wished me to go along with her to meet the editor of a leading local paper. Howard did not. There was no elevator, and I had to run back and forth, conveying the altercation.

"She says it's the Will of God that I should go," I panted.

"Well," said Howard, "you run down and tell her I'm nearer to God up here than she is down there, and it isn't."

About a year after this, we were expecting Martha to pay a visit to Ṭihrán, because the United States consul told us he was receiving mail for her. Howard wrote home: "It will be nice to see her again, but I don't think I could stand traveling with her anymore. She always acts as though God were sitting in the cab, running the locomotive; and that makes me nervous."

Mostly, the three of us were congenial enough. I remember how we all laughed and got hysterical once, as we were going home late one night in the rain, and I started telling her about my mother-in-law's—A. Elizabeth Carpenter's—endless, devoted teaching efforts in Santa Paula, California. About her endless difficulties, and the endless meetings in her house, Sunny Slope (now vanished), and the local indifference, and the being denounced from the pulpit, and the few tottering oldsters, somehow scratched from the rocky soil, who would wend their laborious way up to the meetings. It was Howard's fault that we started breaking up, when he began describing what that hill in Santa Paula was doing to the community.

And there were agreeable, off-duty meals together sometimes, real meals, in restaurants. I remember the time when we promised her not to tell about a certain wine eggnog, if she promised not to tell about some peccadillo of our own; and when we gave her some trivial good-bye gift, on her solemn word that she would not pass it along. There were, too, occasional memorable social visits with distinguished families, like our luncheon with a general and his wife. We had been warned that the undraped female on the dining room wall, selected by the wife for décor, was someone well known to the general, and we found the painting difficult to ignore.

FAR FROM BEING that stereotype—the desiccated spinster—she was concerned about individuals, and had time for them. There was an understated, maternal tenderness about her.

It was this quality in Martha that won over the Persians

(as Keith did not). It was her warmth, her fervor, that surprised the Persians, who to this day consider Americans cold and unfeeling. (Their attitude is illustrated by the following, which they told me in Ṭihrán: "If an American is out walking with a friend," someone assured me, "and his friend falls down, the American will walk right on, saying: 'Time is money. Good-bye.' ")

It was her love which made the young Na'ímí, son of the great Bahá'í poet, write of her: "I have been deeply touched, and have seen the whole audience . . . moved to tears of joy and exultation" at her "simple but impressive words . . . blessed be America . . . which sends us such fervent believers. . . ."[8]

The first time I ever spoke with Martha was in San Francisco, out on the sidewalk after she had addressed the Bahá'ís. Word had just reached me that my grandfather, Francis W. Breed, was dead. I was not accustomed to death, and this was the first break in our family wall.

"My grandfather has died," I said to Martha, a total stranger, surrounded by other members of her audience.

"He has gone into the Kingdom of Light," she answered.

I remember how she kissed Howard good-bye, on his forehead, "because you are sick and your mother is far away." At that time he had two and a half more years to live.

On a later day Martha, with Ella Bailey (who sacrificed her own life in Tripoli), would visit Howard's grave in Berkeley, California, and they would decide to plant a rose tree there.

BY MARZIEH GAIL

IN THE WINTER of 1882–83, President Chester Arthur established the first official link between the United States and Iran, appointing S. G. W. Benjamin as the first ever American envoy to that ancient country.

But decades before this, the Báb had already in effect created such a link, when He had cried out to the "people of the West" to "issue forth from your cities and aid the Cause of God."[9] Certainly an amazing summons from an unknown young merchant, in a country believed by the West to exist only in fables and poems.

Among the early ones to come out of their cities were Laura Barney, my mother Florence Breed, and afterward, Martha—the vanguard of thousands upon thousands who would reply to that summons on a future day.

Such then were the beginnings of the mysterious bond that unites Iran with the United States: Iran, first repository of the Bábí and the Bahá'í Faith—America, cradle of the Bahá'í World Order.[10]

Minister Benjamin's report on his mission[11] is a graphic account of the Persia of that day, and what he saw was much the same as what Ṭáhirih and her fellow "Dawn-Breakers" (the Bahá'í name for the early heroes of this Faith) knew as their accustomed world. This Iran of Benjamin's era was also not far different, in those slow-moving times, from the country as Martha Root found it, or as I knew it myself, during the years I lived there—although, true enough, by the twenties and thirties the jailings and the murderings, however frequent, were less noticeable.

Minister Benjamin tells how the shah, with twelve young

soldiers, tightly bound, cringing in front of him, fixed them with a terrible gaze, but addressed them no word. Standing alone on a portico, leaning with outstretched arm against a pillar, he made a simple gesture with his free hand. Instantly the executioners threw cords around the twelve necks and strangled them before his eyes; and one was slow to die and had to be stamped on.

(Their crime was, the paymasters had stolen their pay, and when they tried to approach the shah's carriage to ask for justice, the paymasters intervened. A few stones struck the royal carriage, and the shah, unharmed, was hurried back to the palace—where the paymasters assured His Majesty that these young men were followers of the new Faith, in a plot against his life).

Martha had read (probably in the works of E. G. Browne) that Ṭáhirih was once brought before this very shah, Náṣiri'd-Dín. No woman remained veiled in the presence of the shah, and he reportedly fixed his gaze upon her and said: "I like her looks: leave her, and let her be." (p. 62) If so, "Let her be" can also mean, "Let her live."

To sum up, all life, and all property, was in the hands of the one man, and the nation was governed by dread. I once asked a Persian woman: "Who does Persia belong to?"

"Why—the shah," she replied.

But there was a catch to it all: while the shah ruled as he pleased, he was only the temporary trustee of the Hidden Imám, who had vanished through a hole in Samarra a thousand years gone. The Hidden Imám, said the Shí'ihs, had never died. He would return in the fullness of time to take over from the shah, and he would rule the whole earth.

The Persia of Ṭáhirih's day was thus a church-state, the clergy intervening cradle-to-grave in every phase of the country's life, the people abject slaves to this "turbaned class.'' It was these who fought to keep women veiled and subjected and unschooled; religious minorities identified by a distinctive badge or dress; the ''unclean foreigners'' (on whose payrolls they often were—the money, at least, was as good as anyone else's) safely at bay.

Their doctors forbade the translation of the Qur'án into Persian, pronounced on the law and saw their capricious decrees carried out, fought the civil tribunals superseding their own, protected the temporary concubinage system which had made Mashhad, center of Persian pilgrimage, ''one of the most immoral cities in Asia.''[12] They betrayed and brought on the destruction of the heroes at Ṭabarsí, they bastinadoed the Báb and Bahá'u'lláh, they signed the Báb's death warrants, they leveled their ''spears of hatred at the face of Bahá.''[13]

And as a mullá wended his way through town on donkey-back, his willing Muslim victims would rush to kiss, not only both his hands but also the tail of his mount.

This world of the Shí'ih ecclesiastics was the world of Ṭáhirih, girl child of the leading mujtahid,[14] in her home city of Qazvín.

OF THE QÁJÁR SHAHS who relate to our Faith, Faṭh-'Alí died in 1834, when Ṭáhirih was seventeen. He was the one with a long black beard, the one with a thousand wives and a carapace of priceless jewels. Next came Muḥammad Sháh, whose envoy to the Báb became a convert, and who had resolved to kill Bahá'u'lláh when he himself died in 1848. Then came the shah who ruled almost fifty years, always in close league with the clergy—Náṣiri'd-Dín, who had sworn to destroy our Faith, and is answerable for the death of untold thousands of believers. Bahá'u'lláh called him the "Prince of Oppressors," and prophesied that he would be made "an object-lesson for the world"; for we remember that Bahá'u'lláh was born to establish justice in a world where it had never been before, and had said, as the Spokesman for the Unseen, "O Oppressors on earth! Withdraw your hands from tyranny, for I have pledged Myself not to forgive any man's injustice."[15] This was also the shah who kept out modern ideas, and who commented: "I want men around me who don't know whether Brussels is a city or a cabbage."[16]

He was assassinated on the eve of his jubilee, shot dead in a holy shrine by a follower of the Afghan Jamálu'd-Dín, propped up in his closed carriage, and—between obsequiously bowing multitudes—driven back at a gallop to Ṭihrán.

Next, the ailing Muẓaffari'd-Dín opened Iran's first Parliament and died (1906). And then, England and Russia in effect divided the country between them, their famed Convention of 1907 beginning with a solemn agreement to respect Persia's "strict independence and integrity."

And soon after, hoping to arouse American business interest in Iran, which was also the stated wish of 'Abdu'l-Bahá,[17] my father, Ali-Kuli Khan, then representing Persia at Washington, selected and sent over W. Morgan Shuster, to reorganize the country's finances (1911). Shuster lasted eight months, was driven out, and wrote a book called *The Strangling of Persia.*

Next on the throne, Muḥammad-'Alí Sháh had gone to war on the Parliament, attacked and bombarded it, been exiled (and would eventually die of boredom in a long yellow palace on the Bosporus). The boy king, Aḥmad Sháh, the plump one on the stamps, replaced him in 1909. He spent much of his time weight-watching in Europe, while his brother, the Crown Prince Regent, ruled.

Next, the Qájár dynasty was itself wiped out by the first Pahlaví shah, in 1925, who also toppled down the age-old Persian rock-wall of Shí'ih Islám. The rule of the hierarchs was ended, and those who think otherwise at this date should remember the words of 'Abdu'l-Bahá, that "the doctors of Persia have no administrative capacity."[18] For today, despite the fundamentalist masses, the significant elements in Muslim Iran are secularized nationalists, not practicing believers.

By Martha's time, the late twenties, early thirties, the Qájár dynasty was gone. The fair skins and long, slanted eyes, with the unbelievable long lashes, of those philoprogenitive royals survived most noticeably in the populace, whose saying was, "Camels, fleas and princes exist everywhere."[19] By her day, in the countryside north of Ṭihrán, there were those great, lonely, leftover palaces, mocking in their emptiness and decay the old-time Qájár magnificence, left now to a caretaker or so, huddled with his family in some abandoned room.

And when Martha saw what was left of Ṭáhirih's house, and knelt and kissed her floor, it too was a phantom now. But perhaps it once had been like a room nearby, which Minister Benjamin describes: "The rafters of the ceiling were carved, and painted blue and scarlet, picked out with gold; the floor was covered with rich carpets, and in the centre was spread a long array of dishes piled with confectionery."[20] Judging by his account, the Qazvín of Ṭahirih's time, which may have had forty-thousand inhabitants, was a green oasis, all quivering with mirage. It was known for its fruit orchards, its pistachios and wines. Its streets were tree lined, with hurrying water courses to either side.

As for the ladies, Ṭáhirih's companions, who once lived

in those rooms, those walled courtyards with their pools and fragrant plants, they could sew seed pearls on velvet, and peel a fruit so it looked like a carved flower. They could not read or write, but they could send for a magician to find a lost object, or provide them with a spell to win their (shared) husband's love. (The marriage age was nine—compare the Church's often disregarded twelve in the Middle Ages). They could buy cannily in the bazaars, have parties in the ḥammám or in other great houses, and give birth every year, each infant at once consigned to a servant's arms. They did not play music or dance—you hired that done. They could carry on feuds. Age set in early, and from then on they mostly complained, until death.

They haunt one still, those long-dead, veiled and scented ladies with their whispering voices. They lived under stars so bright they could have read by them, if they could have read. They breathed the clear, sweet air of Iran's high plateau. At dawn they would go out in the shadowy courtyard and pick the white jasmine blossoms off a dew-laden bush. They lived in a great silence; could hear bird songs interrupting, or sudden, galloping hooves out in the lane, or from beyond the city walls, some high-soprano shepherd boy wailing over never-attainable love. They would let the blue swallows fly in and out of their high-windowed rooms.

WHEN I FIRST SAW this book of Martha's, I wondered why, exactly, she had chosen Ṭáhirih for her theme.

True, Martha was the herald of a Faith that stands for equality of the sexes—but it also addresses all the other problems of our time. Martha stood up for sex equality as does

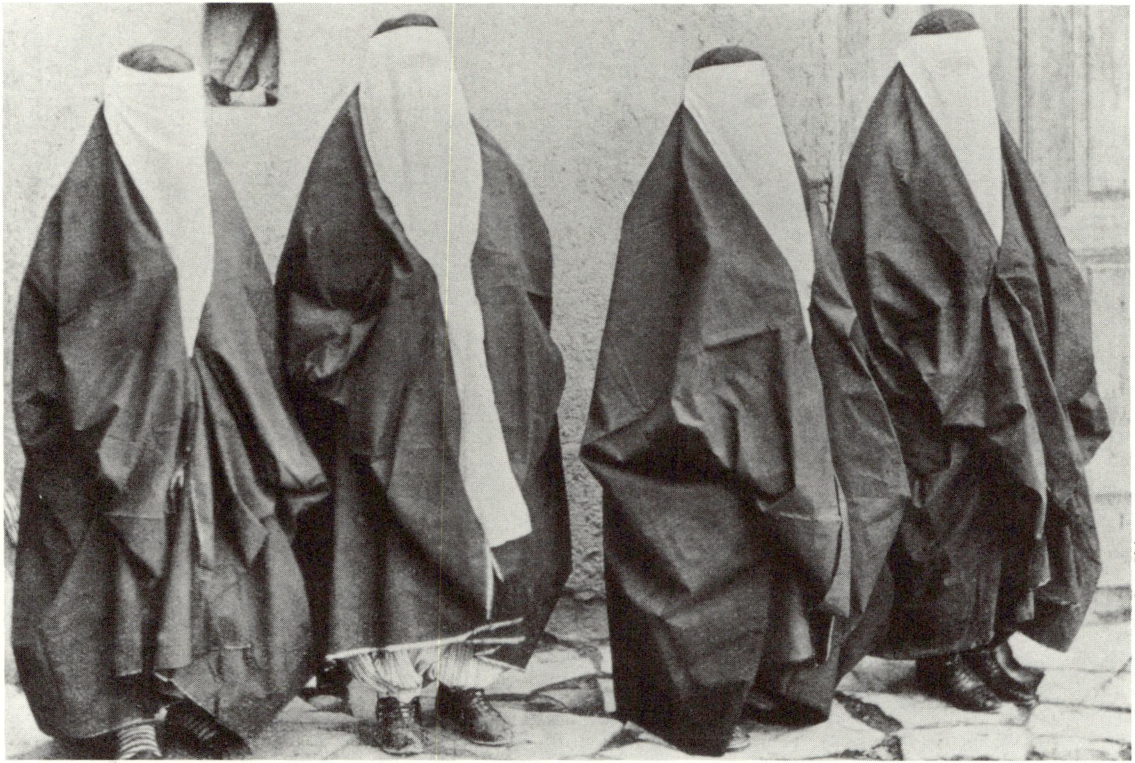

Historical Picture Service, Chicago

PERSIAN WOMEN
wearing the traditional veil

every Bahá'í, but she did not, so far as I could see, single out this principle any more than the others.

So I tried to discover what there was between these two women, born half a century apart, one in a forgotten corner of the East, one in America's Middle West. Between these two who never met—the one whom they likened to Fáṭimih, "Our Lady of Light," daughter of Muḥammad, the Prophet —and the other, Martha, to whom history offers no counterpart.

Finally I set down two columns, one headed Ṭáhirih, the other Martha, and tried to compare them. At first they seemed quite irrelevant, one to the other.

Ṭáhirih, an acknowledged beauty, a man's woman, using cosmetics, scent, wearing pretty clothes; Martha, physically plain and unobtrusive, soberly dressed, never married. Ṭáhirih, famed scholar, impassioned poet, wielding words that cast a spell; Martha, plain in her speech too, and unembellished. Ṭáhirih, who had "second sight" (p. 3); Martha, relying mostly on guidance. Ṭáhirih, who converted many; Martha, a herald and proclaimer of the Faith rather than a confirmer of many souls. Ṭáhirih, who rose up and denounced the evils of her day, who dared to wear bright-colored dresses during the S͟hí'ih days of mourning; Martha, no denouncer, stressing only her great Message. Ṭáhirih, confined to a relatively limited area of the Middle East; Martha, who laboriously circled the whole world four times.

Ṭáhirih, the bold, the impetuous, who dared to appear in that all-male gathering at Badas͟ht, to flout the reverence in which they had held her before—with her charming face unveiled, and her voice upraised to proclaim the new day and the equality of men and women, knowing she must, sooner or later, pay for it with her life. Ṭáhirih, who said to her captors: "You can kill me as soon as you like, but you cannot stop the emancipation of women." (p. ii) Martha, who did not crusade for this or that Bahá'í principle, but for all.

Ṭáhirih, born to the world of the Qur'án—a Holy Book which grants more rights to women than does either the Old Testament or the New, but rights which the men have long perverted and usurped, (the women being unaware, and believing their priests, who told them that women have no souls); but still a Holy Book which places the man above them.[21] Martha, born to Christendom, raised in a long tradition of struggle for women's rights (Mary Wollstonecraft, with her "Vindication of the Rights of Women," 1792; Elizabeth Cady Stanton, with her First Women's Rights Convention, 1848, only days after Badasht; Emily Davison, who in 1913 killed herself for women's sake, broke through the barriers at Epsom race track to die under the hooves of the king's horse). But a Christendom that inevitably must, according to its own Scripture, subjugate woman to man, as man to God: for our new Faith out of Iran is the only religion that grants equality to both.

Ṭáhirih, who had to address the men from behind a curtain; Martha, who could talk face to face with a king. Martha, who died at sixty-seven of a dreaded illness, after long agony; Ṭáhirih, born the same year as Bahá'u'lláh, and who never lived to grow old, murdered out beyond the enameled tile gates of Ṭihrán, in a dark Persian garden by dead of night. Martha, under her rainbow shower tree in Honolulu; Táhirih, down in that lost well, her delicate bones under a heap of rocks.

Somehow, though, we can come through Martha to Ṭáhirih, and through Ṭáhirih to Martha; for after a while I could see where they were alike. When Martha writes of Ṭáhirih's "fidelity in searching for the truth," she is telling us something of her own past. When she describes how

Táhirih was "devotedly carrying out all her divine duties," she could be summing up the days of her own life.

Again, as Martha saw the years closing down, perhaps she wanted another messenger to go on through the world in her stead, awakening the sleeping people, and she had noted the impact of Ṭáhirih's name "in all the five continents I have visited," (p. 83) and so chose Ṭáhirih for her spokesman when her own voice should be still.

"My soul thrilled to understand her!" Martha cries. And thus she became the first from the West to seek out Ṭáhirih's house in old Qazvín, and kneel and kiss the floor of her room. And thus she brings the past alive with the notes on her personal search, her visit to the home place, her long conversations with Ṭáhirih's kin.

Again I thought, Ṭáhirih was a heroine, first of all the women in the Dispensation of the Báb; and Martha was the "star-servant" and she felt an affinity for stars. In this book she reached out to Ṭáhirih, as she had reached out to a reigning queen.

As for what I see to be exactly the same in both: their implacable, never-deviating, undeflectible resolve. Their eyes (the beauteous, great black ones, the lovely, wide-spaced blue-green) fixed forever on one single goal: to herald far and wide the birth of the New Day.

And again, as Quddús would put it, I thought how both of them won "affliction's jewel." (p. 58). And remembered with him that the jewels from that treasure-house are not for everyone.

And then of course there is the fact that both of them went down in history, to glory.

NOTES

1. Shoghi Effendi, *God Passes By* (Wilmette, Ill.: Bahá'í Publishing Committee, 1944), p. 344; Shoghi Effendi, *Messages to America* (Wilmette, Ill.: Bahá'í Publishing Committee, 1947), pp. 39, 30.
2. Shoghi Effendi, *God Passes By,* p. 386.
3. Keith Ransom-Kehler, another outstanding Bahá'í teacher. She was designated by Shoghi Effendi as the first American Bahá'í martyr. She died in Iran in 1933.
4. Shoghi Effendi, *God Passes By,* p. 388.
5. "Truth, truth, above all!"
6. 'Abdu'l-Bahá, *The Promulgation of Universal Peace,* 2 vols. (Wilmette, Ill.: Executive Board of Bahá'í Temple Unity, 1921 and 1922), Vol. 2, p. 276.
7. See Shoghi Effendi, *God Passes By,* pp. 389–93.
8. *Star of the West* 21 (1930): 32.
9. Shoghi Effendi, *God Passes By,* p. 23.
10. Shoghi Effendi, *The Advent of Divine Justice* (Wilmette, Ill.: Bahá'í Publishing Trust, 1963), pp. 15–16.
11. S. G. W. Benjamin, *Persia and the Persians* (Boston: Ticknor & Co., 1887).
12. Shoghi Effendi, *God Passes By,* p. 97.
13. Nabíl-i-A'ẓam (Muḥammad-i-Zarandí), *The Dawn-Breakers: Nabíl's Narrative of the Early Days of the Bahá'í Revelation,* trans. and ed. Shoghi Effendi (Wilmette, Ill.: Bahá'í Publishing Trust, 1932), pp. 320, 372, 510; Shoghi Effendi, *The Promised Day Is Come* (Wilmette, Ill.: Bahá'í Publishing Trust, 1965), p. 85.
14. A doctor of Islamic law.
15. Shoghi Effendi, *God Passes By,* p. 225; Bahá'u'lláh, *The*

Hidden Words of Bahá'u'lláh (Wilmette, Ill.: Bahá'í Publishing Trust, rev. ed., 1954), p. 64.

16. Sir Percy Sykes, *History of Persia,* 3rd ed. (London: Macmillan, 1930), p. 142.
17. 'Abdu'l-Bahá, *The Promulgation of Universal Peace,* Vol. I, p. 32.
18. Edward G. Browne, *A Traveller's Narrative (Makála-i-Shakhṣí Sayyáḥ) Written to Illustrate the Episode of the Báb* (Cambridge University Press, 1891), p. 6.
19. We add that it was polite, Victorian Lord Curzon who changed the original "lice" in this proverb to the more seemly "fleas." (Cf. Nabíl-i-A'ẓam, *The Dawn-Breakers,* p. xl.)
20. Benjamin, *Persia and the Persians,* p. 40.
21. Qur'án 4:38.

ṬÁHIRIH THE PURE

TO

BAHÍYYIH KHÁNUM

THE GREATEST HOLY LEAF

this work is reverently, tenderly dedicated.

INTRODUCTION

TO UNDERSTAND THE STORY of Ṭáhirih, one should know something of the Iran of her time, and should be cognizant of that phenomenal quickening of religion known as the Bahá'í Faith which had its rise in that land in the middle of the nineteenth century. Until then women all over the world were in a state of more or less subjection; now women—and they constitute one-half of the whole human race—after centuries of somnolence, are wide awake to their new position and are stirring to new ideas. It should be of thrilling interest to them to know that the first women's rights martyr was not a Westerner at all, but a young woman poet, Ṭáhirih, sometimes known as Qurratu'l-'Ayn, of Qazvín, Iran.

'Abdu'l-Bahá expressed eloquent tribute to her. I remember so well His words to us in the West: "Amongst the women of our own age is Qurratu'l-'Ayn, the daughter of a Muslim priest. At the time of the appearance of the Báb she showed such tremendous courage and power that all who heard her were astonished. She threw aside her veil despite the immemorial custom of the women of Iran; and, although it was considered impolite to speak with men, this heroic woman carried on controversies with the most learned men, and in every meeting she vanquished them. The Iranian government took her prisoner. She was stoned in the streets, anathematized, exiled from town to town, threatened with death, but she never failed in her determination to work for the freedom of her sisters. She bore persecution and suffering with the greatest heroism; even in prison she gained believers. To a minister of Iran, in whose house she was imprisoned, she said, 'You can kill me as soon as you like, but you cannot stop the emancipation of women.' At last the end of her tragic life came; she was carried into a garden and strangled. However, she put on her very best robes as if she were going to join a bridal party. With magnanimity and courage she gave her life, startling and enchanting all who saw her. She was truly a great heroine. Today, in Iran, among the Bahá'ís, there are women who also show unflinching courage and who are endowed with poetic insight. They are most fluent and speak before large gatherings of people."

Ṭáhirih's courageous, deathless personality forever will stand out against the background of eternity, for she gave her life for her sister women. The sweet perfume of her heroic selflessness is diffused over all the five continents. People of all religions and of none, of all races, and all classes to this day cherish the attar of her deeds, and weep tears of love and longing when her great poems are chanted. Through her fearless stand the balance is shifting, man and woman are becoming more equal. Force, the old standard, is losing its dominance, and intuition, insight, glimpses of cosmic consciousness, and the spiritual qualities of love and service in which woman is strong are gaining ascendancy. And you see that this new epoch is an age in which masculine and feminine elements of civilization are becoming more evenly adjusted. Man and woman are as the two wings of the bird of humanity. This bird cannot attain its highest flight until these two wings are equally strong and equally poised. One of the important teachings of the Bahá'í Faith is that women should be regarded as the equals of men and should enjoy equal rights and privileges, equal education, and equal opportunities. Ṭáhirih had to die for these great ideals, but today our task is to live for them.

Dear readers, no words of mine can portray nearly as well the times in the Iran of the nineteenth century, when Ṭáhirih lived, as the illuminating searchlight picture of that age which Shoghi Effendi, Guardian of the Bahá'í Faith in Haifa, Palestine, has presented in his masterly introduction to his historic book, Nabíl's Narrative, *The Dawn-Breakers.*[1]

So with his most gracious permission I shall use excerpts from his preface:

"The Bahá'í Movement is now well known throughout the world, and the time has now come when Nabíl's unique narrative of its beginnings in darkest Persia will interest many readers. . . .

"The main features of the narrative (the saintly heroic figure of the Báb, a leader so mild and so serene, yet eager, resolute, and dominant; the devotion of his followers facing oppression with unbroken courage and often with ecstasy; the rage of a jealous priesthood inflaming for its own purpose the passions of a bloodthirsty populace)—these speak a language which all may understand. But it is not easy to follow the narrative in its details, or to appreciate how stupendous was the task undertaken by Bahá'u'lláh and His Forerunner, without some knowledge of the condition of church and state in Persia, and of the customs and mental outlook of the people and their masters. . . .

"There exists in English, however, a literature about Persia in the nineteenth century which will give the Western reader ample information on the subject. From Persian writings which have already been translated, or from books of European travellers like Lord Curzon, Sir J. Malcolm, and others not a few, he will find a lifelike and vivid if unlovely picture of the Augean conditions which the Báb had to confront when He inaugurated the Movement in the middle of the nineteenth century.

"All observers agree in representing Persia as a feeble and backward nation divided against itself by corrupt practices and ferocious bigotries. Inefficiency and wretchedness, the fruit of moral decay, filled the land. From the highest to the lowest there appeared neither the capacity to carry out methods of reform nor even the will seriously to institute them. National conceit preached a grandiose self-content. A pall of immobility lay over all things, and a general paralysis of mind made any development impossible.

"To a student of history the degeneracy of a nation once so powerful and so illustrious seems pitiful in the extreme. 'Abdu'l-Bahá, who in spite of the cruelties heaped on Bahá'u'lláh, on the Báb, and on Himself, yet loved His country, called their degradation 'the tragedy of a people'; and in that work, "The Mysterious Forces of Civilisation," in which He sought to stir the hearts of His compatriots to undertake radical reforms, He uttered a poignant lament over the present fate of a people who once had extended their conquests east and west and had led the civilisation of mankind. 'In former times,' He writes, 'Persia was verily the heart of the world and shone among the nations like a lighted taper. Her glory and prosperity broke from the horizon of humanity like the true dawn disseminating the light of knowledge and illumining the nations of the East and West. The fame of her victorious kings reached the ears of the dwellers at the poles of the earth. The majesty of her kings humbled the monarchs of Greece and Rome. Her governing wisdom filled the sages with awe, and the rulers of the continents fashioned their laws upon her polity. The Persians being distinguished among the nations of the earth as a people of conquerors, and justly admired for their civilisation and learning, their country became the glorious centre of all the sciences and arts, the mine of culture and a fount of virtues. . . . How is it that this excellent country now, by reason of our sloth, vanity, and indifference, from the lack of knowledge and organisation, from the poverty of the zeal and ambition of her people, has suffered the rays of her prosperity to be darkened and well-nigh extinguished?'

"Other writers describe fully those unhappy conditions to which 'Abdu'l-Bahá refers.

"At the time when the Báb declared His Mission, the government of the country was, in Lord Curzon's phrase, 'a Church-State.' Venal, cruel, and immoral as it was, it was formally religious. Muslim orthodoxy was its basis and permeated to the core both it and the social lives of the people. But otherwise there were no laws, statutes, or charters to guide the direction of public affairs. There was no House of Lords, nor Privy Council, no synod, no Parliament. The Sháh was despot, and his arbitrary rule was reflected all down the official scale through every minister and governor to the lowliest clerk or remotest headman. No civil tribunal existed to check or modify the power of the monarch or the authority which he might choose to delegate to his subordinates. If there was a law, it was his word. He could do as he pleased. . . .

"Even when a Sháh wished to make a just and wise decision in any case that might be brought before him for judgment, he found it difficult to do so, because he could not rely on the information given him. Critical facts would be withheld, or the facts given would be distorted by the influence of interested witnesses or venal ministers. The system of corruption had been carried so far in Persia that it had become a recognised institution which Lord Curzon well described as follows: . . .

'Before I quit the subject of the Persian Law and its

administration, let me add a few words upon the subject of penalties and prisons. Nothing is more shocking to the European reader, in pursuing his way through the crime-stained and bloody pages of Persian history during the last and, in a happily less degree, during the present century, than the record of savage punishments and abominable tortures, testifying alternately to the callousness of the brute and the ingenuity of the fiend. The Persian character has ever been fertile in device and indifferent to suffering; and in the field of judicial executions it has found ample scope for the exercise of both attainments. Up till quite a recent period, well within the borders of the present reign, condemned criminals have been crucified, blown from guns, buried alive, impaled, shod like horses, torn asunder by being bound to the heads of two trees bent together and then allowed to spring back to their natural position, converted into human torches, flayed while living. . . .'

"From the beginning the Báb must have divined the reception which would be accorded by His countrymen to His teachings, and the fate which awaited Him at the hands of the mullás. But He did not allow personal misgivings to affect the frank enunciation of His claims nor the open presentation of His Cause. The innovations which He proclaimed, though purely religious, were drastic; the announcement of His own identity startling and tremendous. He made Himself known as the Qá'im, the High Prophet or Messiah so long promised, so eagerly expected by the Muḥammadan world. He added to this the declaration that He was also the Gate (that is, the Báb) through whom a greater Manifestation than Himself was to enter the human realm. . . .

"He was the Qá'im; but the Qá'im, though a High Prophet, stood in relation to a succeeding and greater Manifestation as did John the Baptist to the Christ. He was the

Forerunner of One yet more mighty than Himself. He was to decrease; that Mighty One was to increase. And as John the Baptist had been the Herald or Gate of the Christ, so was the Báb the Herald or Gate of Bahá'u'lláh. . . .

"The cause of the rejection and persecution of the Báb was in its essence the same as the rejection and persecution of the Christ. If Jesus had not brought a New Book, if He had not only reiterated the spiritual principles taught by Moses but had continued Moses' rules and regulations too, He might as a merely moral reformer have escaped the vengeance of the Scribes and Pharisees. But to claim that any part of the Mosaic law, even such material ordinances as those that dealt with divorce and the keeping of the Sabbath, could be altered—and altered by an unordained preacher from the village of Nazareth—this was to threaten the interests of the Scribes and Pharisees themselves, and since they were the representatives of Moses and of God, it was blasphemy against the Most High. As soon as the position of Jesus was understood, His persecution began. As He refused to desist, He was put to death.

"For reasons exactly parallel, the Báb was from the beginning opposed by the vested interests of the dominant Church as an uprooter of the Faith. Yet, even in that dark and fanatical country, the mullás (like the Scribes in Palestine eighteen centuries before) did not find it very easy to put forward a plausible pretext for destroying Him whom they thought their enemy."

The Bábís "were overwhelmed by numbers. The Báb Himself was taken from His cell and executed. Of His chief disciples who avowed their belief in Him, not one soul was left alive save Bahá'u'lláh, who with His family and a handful of devoted followers was driven destitute into exile and prison in a foreign land.

"But the fire, though smothered, was not quenched. It burned in the hearts of the exiles who carried it from one country to another as they travelled. Even in the homeland of Persia it had penetrated too deeply to be extinguished by physical violence, and still smouldered in the people's hearts, needing only a breath from the spirit to be fanned into an all-consuming conflagration.

"The Second and Greater Manifestation of God was proclaimed in accordance with the prophecy of the Báb at the date which He had foretold. Nine years after the beginning of the Bábí Dispensation—that is, in 1853—Bahá'u'lláh, in certain of His odes, alluded to His identity, and His Mission, and ten years later, while resident in Baghdád, declared Himself as the Promised One to His companions.

"Now the great Movement for which the Báb had prepared the way began to show the full range and magnificence of its power. Though Bahá'u'lláh Himself lived and died an exile and a prisoner and was known to few Europeans, His epistles proclaiming the new Advent were borne to the great rulers of both hemispheres, from the Sháh of Persia to the Pope and to the President of the United States. After His passing, His son 'Abdu'l-Bahá carried the tidings in person into Egypt and far through the Western world. 'Abdu'l-Bahá visited England, France, Switzerland, Germany, and America, announcing everywhere that once again the heavens had opened and that a new Dispensation had come to bless the sons of men. He died in November, 1921; and today the fire that once seemed to have been put out forever, burns again in every part of Persia, has established itself on the American continent, and has laid hold of every country in the world. Around the sacred writings of Bahá'u'lláh and the authoritative exposition of 'Abdu'l-Bahá there is growing a large volume of literature in comment or in witness. The humanitarian and spiritual principles enunciated decades ago in the darkest East by Bahá'u'lláh and moulded by Him into a coherent scheme are one after the other being taken by a world unconscious of their source as the marks of progressive civilisation; and the sense that mankind has broken with the past and that the old guidance will not carry it through the emergencies of the present has filled with uncertainty and dismay all thoughtful men save those who have learned to find in the story of Bahá'u'lláh the meaning of all the prodigies and portents of our time.''[2]

CHAPTER I

EARLY HISTORY OF ṬÁHIRIH'S LIFE

HAḌRAT-I ṬÁHIRIH, "Her Highness the Pure One," well-known also by the name Qurratu'l-'Ayn, is the most celebrated woman in Iranian history; she will remain forever immortal. As I have traveled in the five continents, I have seen how her life has influenced women, and men too, throughout the world. I have observed how her poetry is sought by scholars in every land, and I know that among Bahá'ís the life of Ṭáhirih is an ideal that everyone yearns to comprehend and attain. Though from the time she first heard of the coming of the Báb to the time she was martyred for the love of His Truth was a little less than nine years, still every day since then, her glorious life has been to us like a "living teacher."

Picture in your mind one of the most beautiful young women in Iran, a genius, a poet, a learned scholar of the Qur'án and the traditions; think of her as the daughter of a jurist family of letters, daughter of the greatest high priest of her province and very rich, enjoying high rank, living in an artistic palace, and distinguished among her young friends for her boundless, immeasurable courage. Picture what it must mean for a young woman like this, still in her twenties, to arise as the first woman disciple of a Prophet, then you will be able to understand this narrative.

The *Journal Asiatique*[3] of 1866 presents even a more graphic view of Ṭáhirih, the English translation of which is as follows: "How a woman, a creature so weak in Persia, and above all in a city like Qazvín, where the clergy possess such a powerful influence, where the 'ulamás because of their number and importance and power hold the attention of the government officials and of the people, how can it be that in such a country and district and under such unfavorable conditions, that a woman could have organized such a powerful party of heretics? That is the important question which has puzzled many and even the historian of Persia, Sipihr; it was as a matter of fact unparalleled in the past."[4]

Presenting to you the true history of this great young woman, I give you first the titles by which she is known to the world. Bahá'u'lláh gave her the name of Ṭáhirih which means the Pure One; her teacher in Karbilá, Siyyid Káẓim-i Ras͟htí called her Qurratu'l-'Ayn which means Consolation of the Eyes; other names by which she is known are Zarrín-Táj which signifies one crowned with gold; and she was also addressed as Nuqṭih which means the Point. The name her father had given her is never used in history, which shows how powerful was the spiritual nature of her life!

This young Pesian woman had very deep intuition, that gift of insight called "second sight." How often I have observed in history that the saints of God are able to foresee events. Sometimes I have asked myself: "Was Ṭáhirih great enough instantly to say, 'O God, I give my life to establish this Faith among mankind,' or did she too, need to be trained by the Infinite God to long to give her life as a martyr to serve this new universal Revelation? Certainly we know that early in her dazzlingly spiritual career she felt the responsibility of being a follower of the Báb. She writes in one of her earlier poems: "At the gate of my heart I behold the feet of the Host and the tents of calamity!" I feel she did know long before and gave radiant acquiescence to her future martyrdom. Viewed in this light, one can understand her chaste spirit, her matchless courage, not only in the danger to her life, but in her being the first woman in the Eastern Muslim world to dare to lay aside the veil even in brief moments, and in being courageous enough to go to the Badasht Conference to consult with this group of men-followers of the Báb. Fáṭimih did not do more to help her father Muḥammad than did Ṭáhirih to assist in bringing into reality the aim of the Báb.

One can almost hear her words as she addressed this group in Badasht where they had come to consult: first, on how to free the Báb from prison; and second, to decide once and for all whether they were to follow the old Muhammadan laws, or if the Báb had introduced new laws; or if they, as representatives of the organization of the Báb, were to institute new laws suited to the new epoch. She may have said, as she addressed them with uncovered face: "That sound of the trumpet, which ushers in the Day of Judgment and the Resurrection, is my call to you now! Arise, brothers, the Qur'án is fulfilled and a new era has begun! Am I not your sister, and you my brothers? Can you not look upon me as a real friend? If you cannot put out of your mind evil thoughts, (because it was unheard of in that age for a woman not to hide her face behind a heavy veil) how will you be able to give your lives for a great Cause? Are you aware that this old custom of veiling the face was not enjoined by Muḥammad? Have you never heard that the wives of the Prophet Himself, on their journeys, had their faces exposed? Do you not remember that in some matters, Muḥammad was wont to tell His disciples to go and ask His wife? But even if this were the law of Muḥammad, today a great Light has come which changes all! This is the Hour of Resurrection. Let us fill the souls of men with the glory of the Revealed Word. Let us emancipate our women and reform our society. Let us arise out of our graves of superstition and self, and pronounce that the Day of Judgment is at hand; then shall the whole earth respond to freedom of conscience and new life. The blast of this trumpet of the Resurrection, it is I!''

On the slender shoulders of the mighty and pure Báb, and His few disciples, fell the task of breaking down an old order of age-long superstitions and customs. This had to be done before the new spiritual civilization could be built upon a firm foundation. Thus it has ever been in the evolution of religion since time immemorial.

Coming from Baghdád to Qazvín, in January 1930, and over the same caravan route which this remarkable heroine of God, Ṭáhirih, had once traversed, entering the city where she was reared, my soul thrilled to understand her! I expressed a wish to see the home in Qazvín where she was born, but friends said it would be impossible. Her relatives are Muslims, and because formerly they were so cruelly angry with her and with the religion inaugurated by the Báb, the world has taken it for granted that this hatred of the Bahá'í Faith still exists.

The owner of the Grand Hotel where I was a guest, standing in his doorway, saw a relative of Ṭáhirih passing. He invited him in, gave him tea and said jokingly, ''Your family ought to be ashamed of yourselves. You are like the black mud out from which the white narcissus sprang. Your ancestor Ṭáhirih is loved in every country of the world, but you people do nothing to show a sign of appreciation. I have an American guest in my hotel who is just longing to see even the house where she once lived.'' The relative replied, ''If she wishes to see Ṭáhirih's home, I'll show it to her!'' ''Oh, no you couldn't,'' said the hotel owner. ''Yes, I can and I will!'' responded the relative; and so it was arranged. I went with

MARTHA ROOT
with some Bahá'ís of Hamadán, Iran

Audio-Visual Department, Bahá'í World Center

MARTHA ROOT
with Bahá'í women of Tabríz, Iran

this hotel owner and the Muslim relative out to the ancient home of this famous young woman. It was a large old place with lovely, intricate lattice work; in its time it must have been one of the finest residences of that part of Iran. This relative showed me the women's wing of the palace where Ṭáhirih had been born, then he took me to a quaint artistic library on the second floor where the little girl sat and studied —the girl who later became a poet and the first woman martyr in Central Asia for the education and equality of women and for laying aside the veil! He showed me the prison, the cellar of the imposing mansion where her father had imprisoned his daughter. But the relative sympathetically explained that Ṭáhirih's father truly loved his gifted daughter, even though he clashed violently with her in religious beliefs. He had incarcerated her in his own home trying to protect her from the savagery of those who were ready to brand her with hot irons because she belonged to the despised Bahá'í Faith, but even he could not save her: they came and carried her away to the city prison.

When I kneeled to kiss the floor of her room and to pray, the relatives all came and stood silently. They were reverent and friendly. As I stepped out from her dear room, this relative said to me, "You are the first Bahá'í who has ever come from the West to ask about Ṭáhirih and see her descendants and her home. I replied, "No one came because he had not the courage. I tell you the truth, we were very afraid of you all!" This good relative though, with tears in his eyes, after the prayer said, "I am not against Ṭáhirih. I feel it is an honor to be a descendant of such a noble family. My mother was the younger sister of Ṭáhirih." He came back with me to the hotel and we had a long talk, and on that day was begun a true friendship between a descendant of Ṭáhirih and a Bahá'í from the West. In the tender, holy memories of

Iran it is sweet to me to see this splendid, kindly lawyer, the relative of Ṭáhirih, standing with the Bahá'ís saying "Alláh-u-Abhá" to me as I motored out from Iran. Spiritually as well as physically he seemed to be standing with them, and in that instant, as though a symbol of the perfect unity, a rainbow gorgeous and bright came into the sky above us!

Remembering many incidents that this relative told me about Ṭáhirih, and having carefully written what descendants of early Bahá'ís told me about her, I present the following sketch. Details differ but all accounts show the same shining glory of this first Bahá'í woman, Her Highness the Pure One. Ṭáhirih was born about 1819 or 1820. The book with the birth records was burned together with her other books and her clothing the day after her tragic death, so I heard; but the consensus of historians and descendants of people who knew her agree that she was born sometime between 1817 and 1820.[5]

As a child she was so intelligent, so eager for knowledge, and so quickly grasped her lessons that her father, one of the most learned mullás of all Iran, taught her himself, and later had a teacher brought in for her. This was most unusual, for girls in her day had no educational opportunities. She outdistanced her brothers in her progress and passed brilliant examinations in all theological studies; few men in her day knew the Qur'án and its meanings and the traditions and Islamic Law as well as she. Because she was a woman they would not give her a degree. Her father said what a pity she had not been born a son, for then she could have followed in his career as a famous mujtahid of the Empire.

Her father's name was Ḥájí Mullá Ṣáliḥ. He had two brothers: the elder was Ḥájí Mullá Muḥammad Taqí, a bitter enemy of the Báb, and the younger Ḥájí Mullá 'Alí, who became a devoted follower of the Báb. Ṭáhirih was married to her cousin Mullá Muḥammad, son of Mullá Taqí, when she was quite young. Some historians state that she was thirteen when she married. Her grandson in Ṭihrán also told me she was thirteen years of age when she was married and that she had three children, two sons and one daughter. He also said that sometime after the death of their mother these children ran away from home because their father was not good to them; one son went to Najaf and the other went to live near Ṭihrán; the girl died not long after the passing of her mother.

Ṭáhirih from her earliest youth was a deep student of religion. One day when she was visiting the home of Mullá Javád's nephew she discovered some books in the library written by two eminent scholars, Shaykh Aḥmad-i Aḥsá'í and his pupil Siyyid Káẓim-i Rashtí. She was profoundly interested in these books and asked to take them home to study them. Some of the relatives of Ṭáhirih told me that she lived most of her life in her father's home and, even after her marriage, she was almost always with her mother until her journeys began. She had a room in her husband's house and a few manuscripts and papers there, and these were not burned after her death. Her host, the cousin, was very loath to loan her the books that day, for he told her that her father, seeing her read them at home, would be greatly displeased, as he was opposed to these modern progressive thinkers. However, she persuaded her cousin-host and took the books to her father's house where she studied them carefully.

I digress a little to explain some of Shaykh Aḥsá'í's teachings because they radically affected the orthodox tenets of Islam which Ṭáhirih had been taught at home. She compared them with the inner principles of the Qur'án and felt that they were sound. One of the tenets of the Shaykh was regarding the belief about the resurrection of the body. He taught that the body will not rise but disintegrate, while the spirit will ascend to heaven and dwell in the presence of God. A second doctrine was that God, in the past, had always sent Teachers or Educators to His people to lead them to His Kingdom, and that this Divine Bounty had not ceased.

Another doctrine of the Shaykh related to the common belief among the Shí'ih Muslims that there was One hidden for a thousand years who would come forth from an underground passage as a great Teacher. Concerning this belief, the Shaykh said that the promised One would not appear like that, but that He would be born of woman, and would manifest Himself very shortly in the world. This last was very important and created a great furor, because for one thousand years the Muslims had been expecting that invisible Person, who, as they believed, had been in hiding, but they were now suddenly told by the Shaykh that He would be born of woman and would come soon!

The mission of Shaykh Aḥmad was to announce the glad tidings that a Báb would come, although he had never seen Him. He also mentioned certain signs of the coming, all of which could be recognized after the appearance of the Báb. A fuller account of these Shaykhís and their doctrines can be found in *A Traveller's Narrative,* Volume II, translated and published by the late Professor Edward G. Browne of Cambridge University, England.[6] Shaykh Aḥmad-i Aḥsá'í was born about 1745.[7] He had left his native place, Aḥsá, in Arabia, and gone to Karbilá and Najaf in Iraq, to teach and diffuse spiritual knowledge; here he later had many followers and attained such fame that Fatḥ-'Alí Sháh of Iran invited him to come to Ṭihrán. During this journey in Iran he stopped in Qazvín. Here he paid a visit to Ḥájí Mullá Muḥammad Taqí. The men had a discussion about the resurrection: the Qazvín mullá called him a heretic, showing such open hostility that Shaykh Aḥsá'í was compelled to leave the city.[8] Ṭáhirih was only a child then, but afterwards, when she used to hear her father and her uncle denounce the doctrines of Shaykh Aḥsá'í, she was heard to say: "The Shaykh is in the right and my father and uncle are in the wrong." They said to her even in those early days: "Read our books and writings; we know better than Shaykh Aḥsá'í."

Ṭáhirih drew all the books she could find about Shaykh Aḥmad's teachings from her cousin's library, and she also asked for and studied the works of Siyyid Káẓim-i Rashtí,[9] the disciple who became the head of the Shaykhí School after Shaykh Aḥmad. It is important to know something of these two great leaders of thought in that period, for just as John the Baptist announced the coming of Jesus Christ, so Shaykh Aḥmad and Siyyid Káẓim foretold the coming of a Báb in the very near future.

Professor Edward G. Browne of Cambridge University writes that Siyyid Káẓim, when a boy of twelve and living in Ardibíl, Iraq, had had a dream in which he was told to put himself under the spiritual guidance of Shaykh Aḥsá'í, who was then residing in Yazd. He went and studied with him and became Shaykh Aḥmad's successor. Siyyid Káẓim wrote more than three hundred books. He died at Karbilá in 1843, just after his return from Káẓimayn. Just before the end he said to some of his disciples, "The time of my sojourn in this world has come to an end, and this is my last journey. Why are ye grieved and troubled because of my death? Do you not then desire that I should go and the true One should appear?" Or as *The Dawn-Breakers* states it: "Is not your love for me for the sake of that true One whose advent we all await? Would you not wish me to die that the promised One may be revealed?"[10]

This spiritual young woman of Qazvín, Ṭáhirih, had been corresponding with Siyyid Káẓim-i Rashtí for some time, asking him many deep questions about religion; and because of her great perception and beauty of character, it was he who had given her the name Qurratu'l-'Ayn which means "Consolation of the Eyes."[11] The letters had been sent and replies received through Ṭáhirih's younger uncle, Ḥájí Mullá 'Alí.

This student of religion tried to present these new teachings to her father, but he only rebuked her. She said that she had found many meanings in these writings, and that all were based on the sayings of the Qur'án and the traditions of the Imáms. She at last said to her father, "I see none of these virtues in you and in Uncle Taqí." She tried to show him the truth about resurrection, ascension, divine promises, and the manifestation of the promised One, but he only spoke against them all. One evening, Ṭáhirih to support her claim mentioned one of the traditions of Imám Ja'far. When the father heard this he was very angry and began to ridicule that tradition. She said to him, "Father, you are criticizing the saying of the Imám!" After that she ceased to speak about religion to her father, but addressed her questions, by letter, to Siyyid Káẓim-i Ra<u>sh</u>tí in Karbilá.

She had a great longing to go to Karbilá to study with Siyyid Káẓim, and her uncle, Ḥájí Mullá 'Alí, helped her and her sister to get permission from the family to make this pilgrimage to the sacred shrines at Karbilá and Najaf; but her real intention was, in addition to making the pilgrimage, to visit her teacher. Perhaps it was easier to get the consent of her father, husband, and her father-in-law because they might have thought that the pilgrimage would bring her back to orthodoxy. Anyway, it is related that these two young women went on a pilgrimage to Karbilá, that both were exceedingly beautiful and ranked among the most noble. Both were rich. There is a village about fifteen miles from

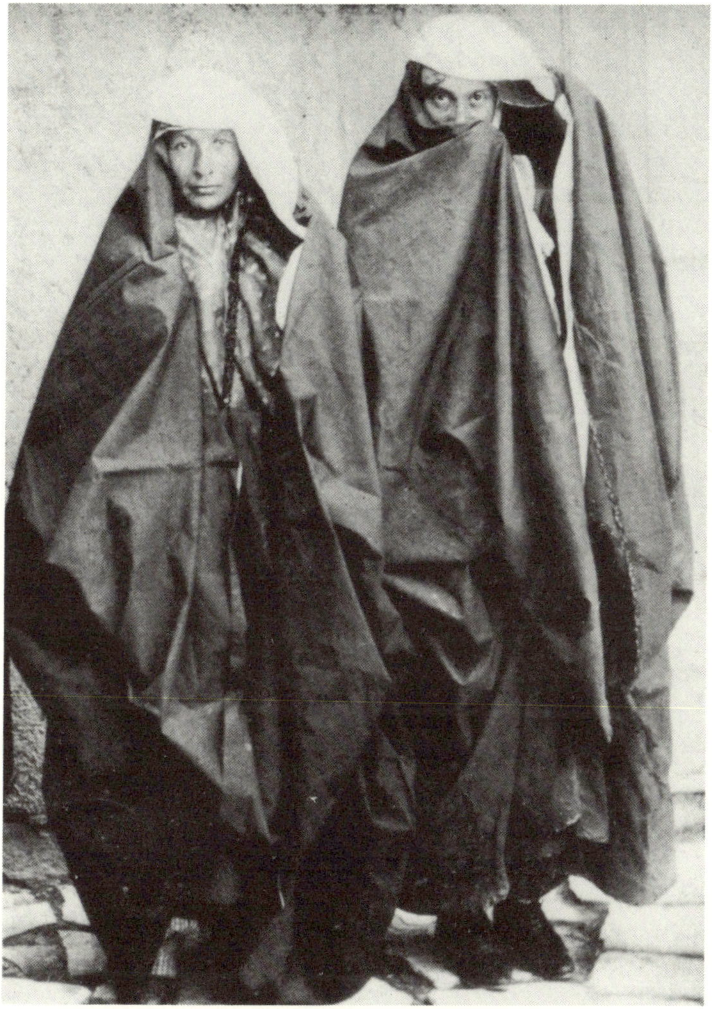

TWO PERSIAN WOMEN
with their veils drawn aside for a photograph

Qazvín which Ṭáhirih's father had given her as one of his gifts; it is called, and the name was chosen by her, Bihjat Ábád, which means "Abode of Happiness."

This journey was made in 1843, when Ṭáhirih was twenty-three years old or as some say, twenty-six, and the mother of two sons and one daughter. Her fame had been well established as one of the most learned young women of the age and one of the most lovely. The only picture one can have of Ṭáhirih is a spiritual one, for no photograph or painting of her was ever made; her relatives told me this. Artists have drawn pictures of her, but they are not from life; they are only imaginary.

During those days she thought only of the coming of the new Teacher into the world; she had told her uncle she wished to be the first woman to serve Him when He appeared. No one realized more than she did the abasement of Iran and the ignorance of woman due to Muslim fanaticism. She said to her uncle, Mullá 'Alí, "Oh, when will the day come when new laws will be revealed on the earth! I shall be the first to follow these new Teachings and to give my life for my sisters!"

Karbilá, and Najaf, which is near to it in Iraq, are the two greatest places for Muslim pilgrimage,[12] except of course Mecca and Medina, in Arabia. However, Ṭáhirih went straight to the house of her teacher Siyyid Káẓim-i Rashtí in Karbilá. Great was her grief to learn that he had passed out from this world ten days before her arrival. She stayed in his home and, through the courtesy of the other members of the household, she had access to his many writings, some of which had never been published. She studied them eagerly and said to his students, "Consider how much Shaykh Aḥsá'í and Siyyid Káẓim-i Rashtí have left us. They have bequeathed to us an ocean of instructions!"

Friends in Baghdád told me that Ṭáhirih remained for three years in Karbilá. Some writers say that she took Siyyid Káẓim's place and began to teach his students. She sat always behind a curtain, for women were not expected to appear without the veil. It was even a remarkable innovation for a woman to permit her voice to be heard outside the harem, the women's quarters. The world knows all too little about the great women who later were so renowned in Iran, women who had their training in part from their close association with Ṭáhirih in Karbilá, and in traveling with her later to other cities. In this group among her students was Shams-i Ḍuḥá;[13] this was a title, her real name was Kurshíd Bagúm of Iṣfahán. She was, or became, the mother of the wife of the King of Martyrs in Iṣfahán and the grandmother of Mírzá Jalál, who married 'Abdu'l-Bahá's daughter Rúhá Khánum of Haifa, Palestine. Other friends were the mother and sister of Mullá Ḥusayn-i Bushrú'í, known as the Bábu'l-Báb because he was the first to accept the Báb. (The title means "the Gate of the Gate.")

'Abdu'l-Bahá, in His *Memorials of the Faithful,* published in the Persian language, has written a short chapter about Ṭáhirih, which is the truest, best account of her life.[14] A devoted Bahá'í in Ṭihrán, Mr. Valíyu'lláh Varqá, courteously read this book aloud to me, translating most of it. Among other points I remember 'Abdu'l-Bahá said that some of the disciples of Siyyid Káẓim-i Rashtí, after the passing of their teacher, went to the Mosque of Kúfih where they were fasting, praying, meditating for forty days. Mullá Ḥusayn Bushrú'í and Mullá 'Alíy-i Bastámí were among these. Others were waiting in Karbilá, and Ṭáhirih was one of these. She kept the fast and meditations during the day, and in the evenings she used to pray and study the religious books. One night, she saw in a dream a young Siyyid standing in the air, then he knelt and prayed. She heard these prayers and learned one by heart, which she quickly wrote down when she awoke.

Some narrators, for example Professor Edward G. Browne in *The New History of the Báb (Táríkh-i-Jadíd),*[15] related that, after the season of prayers by the followers, many of them started out in quest of the promised Báb. Mullá Ḥusayn-i Bushrú'í was leaving for Shíráz. Ṭáhirih told him he would see the promised One and requested her spiritual brother to give the new Teacher her devotion and the letter which she had prepared. When Mullá Bushrú'í met Mírzá 'Alí-Muḥammad in Shíráz, Who announced Himself as the Báb, he became a convert. He gave His Holiness the Báb the letter and message from Ṭáhirih, and then and there the Báb made her one of His Disciples—one of the Eighteen Letters of the Living (and He called Himself the Nineteenth Letter). Thus Ṭáhirih was the first woman to become a believer in the new Faith. The "Kashfu'l-Ghiṭá" announced that Ṭáhirih was informed of the Message of the Báb by Mullá 'Alíy-i Bastámí, who visited Karbilá in the year 1844 A.D. (1260 A.H.) after his return from Shíráz.

However, the account from Nabíl's Narrative, *The Dawn-Breakers,*[16] surely is accurate, and so beautiful that I quote it. "It was she who, having learned of the intended departure of her sister's husband, Mírzá Muḥammad-'Alí, from Qazvín, entrusted him with a sealed letter, requesting that he deliver it to that promised One whom she said he was sure to meet in the course of his journey. 'Say to Him, from me,' she added, ' "The effulgence of Thy face flashed forth, and the rays of Thy visage arose on high. Then speak the word, 'Am I not your Lord?' and 'Thou art, Thou art!' we will all reply." ' "

"Mírzá Muḥammad-'Alí eventually met and recognised

the Báb and conveyed to Him both the letter and the message of Ṭáhirih. The Báb forthwith declared her one of the Letters of the Living." She is the only one of those eighteen disciples, those "Letters of the Living," who never attained the Presence of the Báb—but her inner sight had glimpsed Him first!

Mullá Bushrú'í, it is said, searched out his companion Mullá 'Alíy-i Bastámí who had also come to Shíráz to look for the promised One—the followers from Karbilá had gone in different directions throughout Iran and Iraq but all were seeking the new Teacher. Mullá 'Alíy-i Bastámí, too, accepted the Báb and then he was sent back to Karbilá to carry the Glad Tidings. He took with him one of the Báb's Writings called "The Best of Stories" ("Aḥsanu'l-Qiṣaṣ"), and when Ṭáhirih read this she found in its pages the prayer she had seen in her vision. She was in a state of ecstasy, for now she was quite sure that Mírzá 'Alí-Muḥammad in Shíráz was the new Báb, the Manifestation. She studied the book profoundly, sent for Mullá 'Alíy-i Bastámí and asked him much about the Báb. She believed, and at once began translating into Persian and making comments on this first Book. She also wrote some books in Persian and composed poems about the Báb. She was devotedly carrying out all her divine duties.

When people ask if the Bahá'í Faith arose from Islam, there is only one answer: yes. Just as Christianity sprang from the Jewish religion, so you can see that all the first followers of the Báb were Muslims. Many of them were mullás and the Báb Himself was a direct descendant of Muḥammad. However, His Teachings were *new,* otherwise over three hundred of the greatest mullás in Iran would not have been martyred for this Cause during the first ten years. He called Himself only the Gate of Knowledge to announce "Him whom God shall make manifest.'' Bahá'u'lláh came just as the Báb foretold, and it was Bahá'u'lláh who revealed to this universal cycle the Bahá'í Revelation, a universal religion. It is the greatest truth to know about on the earth today, for it is the master key to this world and the next; and it is the Plan for a new divine civilization.

No thinking man or woman wishes to die without having done something for humanity and for the future generations. Others built for us; surely we are not so indifferent as to fail to look into the most dynamic Plan for the new spiritual development of mankind. Let us study the Teachings for ourselves to see their claims, *prove* them true or false! The finest trait in Ṭáhirih, or at least the one that helped the world most, was her fidelity in searching for the truth. She began as a little girl and continued until the day of her passing from this world.

The ulama, hearing that she had become an ardent believer in the Báb and was teaching this Truth in the very center of Islamic life—for it is in Karbilá and Najaf where many of the world-renowned ulama live—of course complained to the government. Officials in searching for her arrested instead Kurs̲h̲íd Bagúm. As soon as Ṭáhirih learned this, she wrote to the governor saying that she was the one they were looking for, and to release her friend. The governor put Ṭáhirih's house under surveillance, so that no one could come or go; and he wrote to the Bag̲h̲dád government asking for instructions. Guards watched this house for three months so that no one could have access to it. When no word came from Bag̲h̲dád, Ṭáhirih wrote to the Karbilá governor that she was going on to Bag̲h̲dád and would wait there for instructions from the Bag̲h̲dád or Constantinople authorities, for at that time Iraq belonged to Turkey. The governor granted permission and Ṭáhirih, Kurs̲h̲íd Bagúm, and both the mother and sister of the Bábu'l-Báb with many others started for Baghdád. Ṭáhirih was stoned as she was leaving Karbilá.

Reaching Baghdád, the party came to the home of Shaykh Muḥammad ibn Shiblu'l-'Iráqí, the father of Muḥammad Muṣṭafá Baghdádí (Muḥammad Muṣṭafá Baghdádí was the father of Dr. Zia Baghdádí who lived in Chicago for a number of years). Every day, now, she was teaching the Cause. She spoke with such power and eloquence that those who had seen and heard her before were amazed and said, "This is not the woman we knew before." Her lectures began to attract very great audiences; she aroused in her hearers a keen desire to investigate these Truths. Within a short time her extraordinary eloquence, deep learning, and convincing proofs won for her many followers, and a large number of her students in Karbilá came on to Baghdád to attend her classes. As her addresses struck at the very root of the supremacy of the ulama, naturally they were wildly alarmed. Many of them rose up against her and against all who believed in these Teachings of the Báb.

Here in Baghdád, just as in Karbilá, she challenged the clergy—through the governor—to come to a public discussion of these new religious questions. She was also corresponding with the mullás in Káẓimayn. They made excuses, refused, and there was such an outcry from these ulama that the government was obliged to send Ṭáhirih, with the other ladies, to the house of the muftí (judge) of Baghdád. His name was Ibn-i-Alúsí, and he was the son of Siyyid Maḥmúd Alúsí. This was the year 1263 A.H. (1847 A.D.). She stayed there for three months, and all this time they were waiting for instructions from the capital as to what should be done with Ṭáhirih. The muftí each day asked questions along scientific lines, and he did not show any amazement at Ṭáhirih's answers. It is reported that he said:

"O Ṭáhirih! I swear by God that I share in thy belief, but I am apprehensive of the swords of the family of 'Uthmán." Then she went to the house of the chief muftí and there defended her Faith.

During these days in Baghdád many people continued to come to hear about the Teachings. While in Ṭihrán I heard from Dr. Arisṭú Ḥakím how his grandfather, Dr. Ḥakím Masih, physician to the sháhansháh came with His Majesty on a pilgrimage to Karbilá. En route, in Baghdád, this devout Jew, Dr. Ḥakím Masih, so loved by the royal family, saw a large group of very learned people, most of them ulama, listening to a lecture and later conversing with a lady sitting behind a curtain. He went to listen. She was arguing with these mullás. Her speech was so logical she conquered them and they were not able to answer her proofs. He was very astonished, but soon he too was convinced she was right, and he believed! He had not heard of the Báb and he thought this lady must be the promised One. He listened to her lectures three times, continued his pilgrimage with the shah, and returned to Ṭihrán. He offered his services to go to see a very sick man, Mullá Asdaq, imprisoned in a Ṭihrán dungeon for being a Bábí, and from that man learned about Ṭáhirih and the Báb. The many hundreds of Bahá'í Jews in Ṭihrán and Hamadán today are the fruits of his teaching the Jews. His son continued his work, and his grandchildren, most of whom are physicians, are among the most cultured, capable, faithful Bahá'í workers of Ṭihrán today. One grandson Dr. Luṭfu'lláh Ḥakím spent some time with 'Abdu'l-Bahá in Haifa, and was there when the latter ascended on November 28, 1921. To Dr. Luṭfu'lláh Ḥakím we were indebted for the photogaphs of the occasion when 'Abdu'l-Bahá was knighted, His last days in the gardens, and His funeral cortege. Oh, how the Ḥakím family has served this holy Cause since its earliest days![17]

It is attributed to the chief muftí, who entertained Ṭáhirih in Baghdád (at the request of the governor), that he wrote a book in Arabic which is widely read in the East, and in it he speaks of Ṭáhirih during her stay in his home. He said that every morning in the early dawn she would arise and engage in prayer and meditation. She fasted frequently. He stated that he had never seen a woman more virtuous, more devoted, nor any man more learned or more courageous than she was.

One evening the muftí's father came to call upon his son. He did not even greet Ṭáhirih, but began to rebuke his son. The father also said that a message had just arrived from Constantinople in which the sultan gave Ṭáhirih her freedom but commanded her not to stay in Turkish territory. "Make preparations to leave Iraq tomorrow," he instructed her.

Immediately Ṭáhirih and the ladies left the muftí's house and prepared for their journey to Iran. My friends in Baghdád said that this son of Álusí admired Ṭáhirih for her learning. They told me that he said, "I see in her such knowledge, education, politeness, and good character as I have not seen in any great men of this century." The Baghdád friends said that when his father entered the house and began cursing Ṭáhirih because he felt she had changed the religion of Muḥammad, his son was ashamed and came to ask Ṭáhirih's pardon, begging her to forgive the fault of his father. It was he himself, the muftí, who came to tell her, "You are free, but now you must arrange your things for traveling to Iran, for the sultan commands it."

A large group of friends, more than thirty in all, went with her on her journey, for they loved her and realized the dangers ahead. The muftí of Baghdád graciously sent ten horsemen under the command of a general who, with great honor and respect, escorted her with her friends from Baghdád to Khíniqín and to the Persian frontier. With her exalted Highness Ṭáhirih were Kurshíd Bagúm and the mother of Mírzá Hádíy-i Nahrí; others were Siyyid Aḥmad-i Yazdí, Siyyid Muḥammad-i Báyigání, Siyyid Muḥsin-i Káẓimí, Mullá Ibráhím-i Maḥallatí, among the Persians; and among the Arabs were Shaykh Muḥammad-i Shibl who arranged everything for her journey, hiring the mules and the places to sit, ordering the food and he paid all the expenses for the group as far as Kirmánsháh. Others from Iraq were his son Muḥammad-Muṣṭafá, Shaykh Ṣáliḥ-i Karímí, Shaykh Sulṭán-i Karbilá'í, Darvísh Makú'í, Javád, 'Abdu'l-Hádíy-i Zahrawí, Ḥusayn-i Hallawí, Siyyid Jabbání, and others.[18]

When Ṭáhirih and her friends reached Kirmánsháh the women were given one house and the men another. As soon as the inhabitants heard of their arrival they rushed to hear about the Teachings. The ulama created an uproar and caused their expulsion; the mayor of Kirmánsháh permitted a mob to attack their houses and loot everything the Bábís possessed. Then these followers of the Báb were put into a coach drawn by horses, and they were driven out into the desert. There they were put out. The coach was left but the horses were taken back to the city. These travelers were in a miserable condition. They had no food, no change of clothing, no rugs. Ṭáhirih wrote to the governor of Kirmánsháh, explaining what the mayor had done, and she added: "We were your guests in Kirmánsháh; do you think it was kind to treat us like this?" One of the group walked to Kirmánsháh to take this message.

When the governor received her letter he was very surprised, for he had known nothing about this injustice. He found that all had been done at the instigation of the ulama and at once commanded the mayor to return all pillaged property to these people, to take the horses back to them, and see that they could go safely on to Hamadán. He even invited them to return to Kirmánsháh, but this Ṭáhirih declined to do. According to *The Dawn-Breakers,*[19] an enthusiastic reception was accorded her on her arrival in Kirmánsháh. Princes, ulama, and government officials hastened to visit her and were greatly impressed by her eloquence, her fearlessness, her extensive knowledge, and the force of her character. The Commentary on the Sura of Kawthar, revealed by the Báb, was publicly read and translated. The wife of the amír, the governor of Kirmánsháh, was among the ladies who met Ṭáhirih and heard her expound the sacred Teachings. The amír himself, together with his family, acknowledged the truth of the Cause and all testified to their admiration and love for Ṭáhirih. According to Muḥammad Muṣṭafá,[20] Ṭáhirih tarried two days in the village of Ṣaḥnih on her way to Hamadán, where she was accorded a reception no less enthusiastic than the one which had greeted her in the village of Karand. The inhabitants of the village begged to be allowed to gather together the members of their community and to join hands with the body of her followers for the spread and promotion of the Cause. She advised them, however, to remain; she extolled and blessed their efforts, and proceeded to Hamadán.

So the journey was continued and along the way, especially at Ṣaḥnih, chiefs of tribes welcomed her. When they reached Hamadán all were very happy; they were given a reception of welcome. The governor came to visit her and to hear about the Teachings; princesses and other notable women came to listen to her.

No wonder they were eager to speak with her, for she brought the Truth, and as the late Professor Edward G. Browne of Cambridge University, said, "The appearance of such a woman as Ṭáhirih in any country and in any age, is a rare phenomenon, but in such a country as Iran it is a prodigy

—nay, almost a miracle. Alike in virtue of her marvelous beauty, her rare intellectual gifts, her fervid eloquence, her fearless devotion, and her glorious martyrdom, she stands incomparable and immortal amidst her countrywomen. Had the religion of the Báb no other claim to greatness, this were sufficient—that it produced a heroine like Qurratu'l-'Ayn [Ṭáhirih].''

One of the leading mullás of Hamadán, however, was very much opposed to Ṭáhirih and would have urged the people to kill her, but he feared the government. She wrote him a long letter explaining the Teachings of the Báb and sent this to him by one of the faithful disciples, Mullá Ibráhím-i Maḥallátí. He brought it just at an hour when several ulama had met to decide what they could do against Ṭáhirih. This letter was like a red flag to a bull. They fell upon its bearer, Mullá Ibráhím, and beat him until he became unconscious. When he was brought back to Ṭáhirih, she did not weep as the princesses feared she would do, but she astonished them all by saying, ''Come, get up, Mullá Ibráhím. Happiness and peace be upon your that you have suffered in the path of your Beloved! Rise up, and continue to work for Him!'' When he opened his eyes, Ṭáhirih smiled at him and said, ''O Mullá Ibráhím, for one beating you became unconscious; this is the time we are ready to give our lives. Did not the disciples of Christ do it, and the disciples of Muḥammad?'' And Mullá Ibráhím actually arose from his faint and began to serve again.

Ṭáhirih was planning to go to Ṭihrán to try to meet His Imperial Majesty Muḥammad Sháh and tell him about these new Teachings, but one of the mullás, who had refused to meet her and discuss the new religion when she was in Kirmánsháh, had secretly written to her father to tell him that his daughter was disgracing the reputation of the mullás.

Her father at once sent his son and some of the other relatives to Hamadán to welcome her but to urge her to return home. Intuitively she knew they were on the way, and she said to her followers, "They are coming for us, so we shall start back to Qazvín before they reach here." She sent a number of her devoted followers back to Iraq. She left some in Hamadán, and a few others acompanied her. Among the latter were Kurs͟híd Bagúm, S͟hayk͟h Ṣáliḥ-i Karímí, and Mullá Ibráhím of Maḥallát. They met the mounted men, her relatives, who had been sent to find her; these wished to take her alone to her father's house. She refused their offer saying, "I am not alone. These are my friends and they must accompany me." So they all remained together. It was bad weather and a disagreeable journey of one week.

CHAPTER II

EVENTS IN QAZVÍN AND ṬIHRÁN

ARRIVING IN QAZVÍN, Ṭáhirih went to her father's home, and the Arabs took a place in a caravanserai. That first night there was a family council, and her father, her husband, and her uncle (who was also her father-in-law) reproached her. In the excitement her father said, "If you, with all the learning, scholarship, and intelligence which you possess, were to claim to be the Báb or even more than that, I would readily admit and allow your claim; but what can I do, when you choose to follow this Shírází lad?" The book *Tárikh-i-Jadíd* has the following: "Great heavens! Such is the arrogance and prejudice of this family that the imagination can scarcely conceive these developments! Here was one who saw his daughter, notwithstanding her talents and accomplishments, regarded herself but as the dust in comparison with that Sun of Truth and publicly said: 'With the knowledge which I possess, it is impossible that I should be mistaken in the recognition of Him who is the Lord of the Worlds, whom all peoples anxiously expect: I have duly recognized Him by the proofs of reason and the evidences of knowledge; though this knowledge and these attainments of mine are but a minute drop beside that vast and all-embracing ocean or as an insignificant mote beside that mighty and radiant luminary'; yet nothwithstanding this, her father answered: 'Though you regard your excellence and learning of such small account in comparison with the virtues of the

S͟hírází lad, still, had you been my son (instead of my daughter) and had you put forward this claim (of being the Báb), I would have accepted it.' ''

Her Uncle Taqí, who, as I said, was Ṭáhirih's father-in-law, cursed the Báb and in his violent anger struck her several blows. With her quick intuition she uttered those fatal words of foresight which later almost caused her to be branded with hot irons. She said, ''O Uncle, I see your mouth fill with blood!''

The question of her returning to her husband arose, and this she absolutely refused to do. Try as they might, she would not consent to be reconciled with her husband Mullá Muḥammad. She gave as her reason: ''He, in that he rejects God's religion, is unclean; between us there can be naught in common.'' Or as *The Dawn-Breakers* states it, Ṭáhirih had replied to his request: ''If your desire had really been to be a faithful mate and companion to me, you would have hastened to meet me in Karbilá and would on foot have guided my howdah[21] all the way to Qazvín. I would, while journeying with you, have aroused you from your sleep of heedlessness and would have shown you the way of truth. But this was not to be. Three years have elapsed since our separation. . . .''[22] This marriage had not been of Ṭáhirih's choosing. Parents in those days arranged the betrothals and marriages. Her husband a few weeks later divorced her. His father and he pronounced her a heretic and strove day and night to undermine her position.

During the first few days after her return, Ṭáhirih used to go to a kinsman's house, where she could meet the wives of distinguished men and speak with them frankly about the Teachings of the Báb. Her brother-in-law and sister were believers. According to Samandar, who was one of the early believers of Qazvín, and whose descendants I met and spoke

THE GATE OF QAZVÍN

with often during my stay in Qazvín, Ṭáhirih's sister, Marḍíyyih, was the wife of Mírzá Muḥammad-'Alí, one of the Letters of the Living. He later suffered martyrdom at Shaykh Ṭabarsí. Marḍíyyih recognized and embraced the Message of the Báb. Mírzá Muḥammad-'Alí was the son of Ḥájí Mullá 'Abdu'l-Vahháb, to whom the Báb addressed a Tablet while in the neighborhood of Qazvín.

Ṭáhirih's and Marḍíyyih's Uncle Taqí was an Imám-Jum'ih, which means that he was the chief of the mullás and led the prayer on Fridays in the mosque. Suddenly, word came that Mullá Taqí had been murdered in the mosque.[23] His son and all the family recalled Ṭáhirih's words: "I see your mouth fill with blood!" and they accused her of instigating the murder or at least of knowing all about it. Yet her mother said, "How could one know so exactly about anyone's death, if she did not get it through vision?" Her mother felt that her daughter was innocent, and this mother and daughter had always been close to each other—relatives of the family told me so.

Here I give you a few paragraphs from Jináb-i Samandar Qazvíní, the old and great Bahá'í who wrote it especially for Dr. Susan I. Moody in Ṭihrán. She had been asked to send something about Ṭáhirih to Mrs. Carrie Chapman Catt, President of the International Women's Suffrage Alliance, for their Congress in Budapest, Hungary, in June, 1913, and later to be published in a book about notable women. It was not received in time by Dr. Moody and thus nothing was sent to Budapest, but this part about the murder is significant because it is an account by one who was a little boy in Qazvín at that time and remembered the event vividly:

"A certain Mullá 'Abdu'lláh Ṣáliḥ of Shíráz, who according to his own statement was not a convinced believer in the Báb, but was a fervent admirer of Shaykh Aḥmad and

Siyyid Káẓim, at that time having heard Ḥájí Mullá Taqí often abuse his friends, went one night to the masjid[24] of Taqí and concealed himself there until morning. When Mullá Taqí came in the morning to pray, this man struck him in the mouth with a stiletto, and then hid the stiletto under a bridge near the mosque and ran away: at that moment no one else save God knew of the deed. When the people gathered for prayer, they understood that Taqí had been attacked and killed. They informed his son and other relatives and bore the body home. God is my witness of what happened that day in Qazvín.

"Because the people thought that Ṭáhirih and the believers had brought about this death, the officers of the government were commanded to arrest prominent believers, and a crowd of theological students entered the house of Ḥájí Siyyid Asadu'lláh.[25] He and his nephew Áqá Mihdí, who were in the house, were arrested and taken to prison.

"The mob plundered the houses of everyone known to be a relative of the believers. I was a very small child but I remember well the time that Siyyid Muḥsin, known as a persecutor and murderer of Bábís, accompanied by many officers and executioners knocked at our door. No one opened it, so they climbed over the wall and entered, investigating and wishing to break into some rooms that were locked. The master of the house opened the doors, while all the family was shaking with fear on account of the horrible actions of these men. This Siyyid Muḥsin would say to the women, 'Your husband has left his religion and this means you can be married to anyone whom you wish.'

"Acting on the suspicion that Ṭáhirih had contrived with Ḥájí Siyyid Asadu'lláh to bring about the death of Mullá Taqí, his son Mullá Muḥammad, who was the husband of Ṭáhirih, induced the governor to put her on trial. Her father refused to let her go, but later they took her by force, with her the maidservant Káfiyih and other women. They were questioned at Government House, but replied, 'This deed has been perpetrated without our knowledge.' Mullá Muḥammad kept urging the governor to punish them severely. Acting on this hint, the governor gave the executioner an order to bring in the irons for branding. In order to terrorize Ṭáhirih they proceeded to put the hands of Káfiyih under a sliding door, intending to brand them from the other side. Her Highness Ṭáhirih, under these terrible conditions, realizing that God was their only refuge, turned her uncovered face toward the prison of the Báb at Máh-Kú, and began to pray and supplicate. At that moment the situation was beyond words.

"Then on the air outside a voice arose, crying: 'The murderer is found!' This turned the attention of all. Who is the murderer and where was he found? No branding was done. It was learned that the murderer was that same Mullá Ṣáliḥ-i Shírází, who, when he beheld the wild commotion in the city and saw the arrest of the innocent, fled on foot to Government House and confessed his crime saying, 'I was the one who thrust the dagger into his mouth. I had no accomplice and you have arrested people of God without cause.'

"They asked him, 'Why did you kill such a learned man?' He answered, 'He was not a learned man; he that only stole a little bunch of grapes from a cultural garden. Had he been a wise man he would not have used evil words in the pulpit against my teachers Shaykh Aḥmad-i Ahsá'i and Siyyid Káẓim-i Rashtí, and for that reason only have I killed him.' Then they brought him into the High Court of Justice face to face with Mullá Muḥammad and Ḥájí Mullá Ṣáliḥ, husband and father of Ṭáhirih. He was examined and put to trial and with great eloquence he made his confession. They said, 'He is lying.' Then he added, 'The stiletto with which I struck him in the mouth is hidden under the bridge near the mosque!'

"A messenger was sent who found and brought the stiletto. Mullá Muḥammad then said angrily, 'This man is not worthy to be the murderer of my father.' Mírzá Ṣáliḥ replied, 'Bring a suit of fine clothes for me so that your father's murderer may appear worthy,' and with heavy chains about his neck he was then taken to prison. The people of the city were coming in groups to peer at him through the windows of the prison. Among them was the aforementioned Siyyid Muḥsin, who as he neared the prison door began abusing him with vile words. Quickly the brave lion sprang toward him, throwing the spike of his chain at him. The Siyyid turned and fled. During this time and while her husband was persecuting the believers and demanding many lives in retribution for his father's life, Her Highness Ṭáhirih was closely confined in her father's house and was entirely prevented from communicating with the world outside.

"Mullá Muḥammad, her husband, and another cousin intended to poison her but they did not succeed. None of the friends could go to the house except Khátún-Ján, the eldest daughter of Ḥájí Asadu'lláh. This devoted and faithful friend was ingenious in finding excuses to go to the house. Sometimes she would get in under the pretense of rinsing clothes, and thus obtain news or carry in food, since Ṭáhirih was often obliged to refuse the food prepared in the house, and thus was sustaining life under great difficulty and hardship. Áqá Muḥammad-Hádí, the husband of this loyal friend, was the eldest brother[26] of Her Highness, and, I have been told, by Jináb-i-Aqá Muḥammad Jawád-i Farahádí (known to all Bahá'ís as Amú-Ján), that this brother, Áqá Hádí, had secretly left Qazvín at the time of the murder of

Mullá Taqí, that he went to Ṭihrán and entered the presence of Bahá'u'lláh, Who sent him back to Qazvín to help Ṭáhirih and bring her to Ṭihrán. He carried a holy letter to her from Bahá'u'lláh, which his wife delivered using the same strategy as before.

"After reading the letter Ṭáhirih said, 'You go and I shall follow.' And within the hour she started out. They took her to the house of a carpenter, where no one would think of looking for her. However, her absence was soon discovered and at once the city was in an uproar and the house of Ḥájí Asadu'lláh was looted and sacked. During that same night Áqá Hádí with the assistance of Áqá Qulí, a servant and a devoted believer, took her to the city wall near the gate called Sháhzádih Ḥusayn. They succeeded in passing over the wall and went to a slaughterhouse outside the city where horses were waiting. Mounting them, they started for Ṭihrán, going by way of the villages Kuldarih and Ishtihárd. When they reached the Shrine of the Imám-Zádih Ḥasan, four miles from Ṭihrán, they stopped for the first time. Áqá Qulí cared for the horses while Her Highness was resting, and Áqá Hádí went into Ṭihrán to make known her arrival. A believer named Karbilá'í Ḥasan went out to the garden to see her, but as Áqá Qulí did not know him he refused to let him enter. He smilingly persisted and Áqá Qulí gave him two hard blows on the chest. Her Highness here came to the rescue and brought the guest fruit and báqilá—a species of bean—and conversed with him until a party of horsemen came and took them to the house of Bahá'u'lláh.[27]

"The next day she was taken to a village where there were many believers. Áqá Qulí was rewarded abundantly for his faithfulness; he prospered in all his affairs, later becoming a high official in the government. He also made a pilgrimage to the presence of Bahá'u'lláh, but of this I have not the

Historical Picture Service, Chicago

THE BAZAAR
An artist's fanciful conception of the bazaar of Ṭihrán, circa 1873

detailed account, neither do I know by what means Her Highness was later brought back to Ṭihrán nor the actual facts of her martyrdom. (Signed) Samandar."

Mírzá Ṣáliḥ-i S͟hírází, the murderer of Mullá Taqí, was put in chains and sent to Ṭihrán. After reaching Ṭihrán (and some historians say it was before he left Qazvín) he learned that although he had confessed his crime in order to save the believers they were not released. So one night he escaped from his prison and took refuge at the house of Riḍá K͟hán, the son of the Master of the Stable of Muḥammad S͟háh. Riḍá K͟hán was a believer. After a few days, with his host Mírzá Ṣáliḥ, who by now had become very attracted to the Cause of the Báb, he fled to the fortress of Ṭabarsí in Mázindarán. Mounted police were sent out from Ṭihrán to search for him, but he reached the fortress in safety.[28]

Some of the other Bábí prisoners were sent back to Qazvín and put to death. The *Táríkh-i-Jadíd* states: "Those innocent persons remained in prison, but though the son of Hájí Mullá Muḥammad-Taqí made the most strenuous efforts to obtain from the administration of the Sacred Law in Ṭihrán an order for the execution of one of the prisoners, he was not successful. Then he accused the believers in the Báb's Teachings of this and that; and His Majesty Muḥammad S͟háh ordered the learned mujtahid Áqá Maḥmúd of Ṭihrán to investigate and ascertain their tenets. So they brought the prisoners before him, and when he had met and conversed much with them, the falsity of Mullá Muḥammad's assertions concerning the Bábís became evident. Finally, Mullá Muḥammad went before His Majesty the Shah and rent his shirt, and began to weep, saying, 'They have slain Ḥájí Mullá Muḥammad Taqí, and shall no one's blood be shed in atonement?' The shah answered, 'The murderer, who has himself confessed, has escaped from prison. If thou desirest the lawful application of the *lex talionis,*[29] then no administrator of the Sacred Law will sentence an innocent man to suffer death instead of the escaped murderer. But if thou seekest for illegal retaliation, then why dost thou introduce the name of law? Go, kill one of them.' So they took Shaykh Ṣáliḥ the Arab, a godly man, endowed, as was proved in several ways, with a pure heart and consummated his martyrdom by blowing him from the mouth of a cannon.

"Then Mullá Muḥammad prayed that he might be permitted some other prisoners (one of whom was Shaykh Ṭáhir of Shíráz the preacher, and the other Mullá Ibráhím of Maḥallát) to take to Qazvín, in order that he might do honor to his father's memory by causing them to walk round his grave, after which he would let them go. To this His Majesty agreed. Some of these were savagely put to death on their way to Qazvín, and in the march round the grave Shaykh Ṭáhir was bound to a tree and tortured to death. Mullá Ibráhím was also cruelly done to death by the incited populace who gathered at the grave for this very purpose. Thus the two early students of Ṭáhirih, Shaykh Ṣáliḥ the Arab, and Mullá Ibráhím were the first believers to shed their blood on Iranian soil in the path of the Cause of God; the first of that glorious company destined to seal with their lifeblood the triumph of God's holy Faith. Ḥájí Asadu'lláh, the older believer in Qazvín who had done so much to help her, died of cold and fatigue on the way to Ṭihrán when they were taking him there as a prisoner.

Ṭáhirih was now a guest in the home of Bahá'u'lláh in Ṭihrán and though search was being made for her, she seemed to be teaching individuals each day, speaking behind a curtain. People were surprised to see so many persons coming and going from Bahá'u'lláh's house, and to note so many believers frequenting his palace. He was the son of a

Minister, His father was at one time chief secretary to His Imperial Majesty the S͟háhans͟háh. I saw Bahá'u'lláh's home in Ṭihrán; it showed that He must have been very rich for it was like seven great residences all connected. Also He had a summer home outside the city on the Elburz Mountain slope. He had become a follower of the Báb, soon after the Bábu'l-Báb, in 1844. He never saw the Báb. The Báb and Bahá'u'lláh corresponded with each other from the time when Bahá'u'lláh accepted the Báb's Cause.

Ṭáhirih, who, as I stated in the beginning, had never seen the Báb, longed to go to Máh-Kú to meet Him. Bahá'u'lláh explained to her how impossible this would be.

The believers had been given permission by the Báb and urged to visit K͟hurásán if possible, to learn from and honor the Bábu'l-Báb. Ṭáhirih decided to do this, but in the days she remained in Ṭihrán she quickly saw the great station, spiritually, of Bahá'u'lláh and consulted Him in all matters. To me it was strange, but certainly when I was in Ṭihrán and spoke with a descendant of Ṭáhirih, he said that she had told the s͟háhans͟háh she believed in Bahá'u'lláh and was commanded by Bahá'u'lláh to proclaim the New Day of God. I repeated my question, asking if he did not mean the Báb, and the second time he answered: "No, it was Bahá'u'lláh!" Certainly with her deep insight she recognized Bahá'u'lláh's part in this great universal religion, and every act of her life after this visit proved it.

She was also very devoted to 'Abdu'l-Bahá, then a little boy three or four years old. She used to hold him a great deal. One day Siyyid Yaḥyáy-i Darabí, surnamed Vahíd, came to call upon her. He was one of those early believers who later was martyred near Nayríz. He waited a long time and friends said to Ṭáhirih, "Should you not leave the child and go and speak with him?" She is said to have replied as she drew the little one closer to herself, "Shall I leave thee, Protector of the Cause, and go to see one of the followers of the Cause?" Those who heard this were amazed, because at that time even the Father of this little boy had not announced His Own Mission. Perhaps in their private talks Bahá'u'lláh had told her something of His work.

'Abdu'l-Bahá in his book *Memorials of the Faithful* also speaks of this visit of Siyyid Yaḥyáy-i Darabí, called Vahíd. He said, "I was sitting on the knee of Jináb-i Ṭáhirih, and Siyyid Yaḥyá was reciting some of the traditions of the Imáms regarding the new Manifestation. Suddenly Ṭáhirih interrupted him and said, "O Yaḥyá, bring forth an act if you have the real knowledge! Today is not the time for reciting traditions, but today is the time for steadfastness, for tearing away the veils of superstition, for uplifting the Word of God, for sacrificing our lives in the Path of God. Indeed we must support our talk with real acts."

The next significant event in the history of the Cause was the Conference at Bada<u>sh</u>t. Perhaps you ask, where is Bada<u>sh</u>t? It is situated between Ṭihrán and Mázindarán, an out-of-the-way summer-place, full of gardens and pastures with a few houses. It used to be a summer resort for the nobility. Nothing is more natural than that Bahá'u'lláh should choose it for the council of the Báb's followers, for it was quiet and had beautiful gardens just outside the place. The three gardens they occupied had a great court or square in the center. There they could consult freely; it was far too dangerous to attempt such a gathering in Ṭihrán. Probably the believers were going to stop in this hamlet, en route to <u>Kh</u>urásán.

Bahá'u'lláh sent Ṭáhirih to Bada<u>sh</u>t with servants and preparations and money for the expenses of all her party. A few days later, He Himself set out, and Quddús also came.

Bahá'u'lláh rented three gardens, one of which He assigned exclusively to Quddus; another He set apart for Ṭáhirih and her attendants; and He reserved the third for Himself. The tents of the believers were pitched in the court in the center. Bahá'u'lláh's tent was that of a noble family, for He was the son of a Vazír. Ṭáhirih's words to one of the servants show the solemn import of this gathering. When she saw that he wondered that she, a woman, was there consulting and addressing—even from behind a curtain—in that first day so many men, she called him to her and said, "Our talk is about God, about religion, about spiritual matters, and above all about surrendering our lives in the path of Truth. Know that every step we take is in the path of God. Are you prepared to follow us?" Each day one of their numbers gave a talk on the Cause of the Báb.

I quote from *The Dawn-Breakers* the following account: "Those who had gathered at Badas͟ht were eighty-one in number, all of whom, from the time of their arrival to the day of their dispersion, were the guests of Bahá'u'lláh. Every day, He revealed a Tablet which Mírzá Sulaymán-i Núrí chanted in the presence of the assembled believers. Upon each He bestowed a new name. He Himself was henceforth designated by the name of Bahá; upon the Last Letter of the Living was conferred the appellation of Quddús, and to Qurratu'l-'Ayn was given the title of Ṭáhirih. To each of those who convened at Badas͟ht a special Tablet was subsequently revealed by the Báb, each of whom He addressed by the name recently conferred upon him. When, at a later time, a number of the more rigid and conservative among her fellow-disciples chose to accuse Ṭáhirih of indiscreetly rejecting the time-honored traditions of the past, the Báb, to whom these complaints had been addressed, replied in the following terms: 'What am I to say regarding her whom the Tongue of

Power and Glory has named Ṭáhirih [the Pure One]?' Each day of that memorable gathering witnessed the abrogation of a new law and the repudiation of a long-established tradition.''[30]

Monsieur A. L. M. Nicolas, the French historian, described this meeting and says it continued for several days. The discussion related mainly to the change from the old religion to the new Teachings of the Báb.

According to 'Abdu'l-Bahá's account in *Memorials of the Faithful,* at the time this meeting was held in Badas͟ht, the Báb had not yet proclaimed the final stage of His Manifestation which was that of Qá'im. He had first declared Himself to be the Báb (Gate), but by Qá'im is meant the promised Imám. Bahá'u'lláh, Quddús, and Ṭáhirih here at Badas͟ht made necessary arrangements for the general proclamation of the Báb and the abrogation of certain formal rights and traditions. Then on a certain day Bahá'u'lláh was ill with fever in His tent, and indeed there was a wisdom in this. Jináb-i Quddús came out of his own garden and went to see Bahá'u'lláh. Ṭáhirih sent word and asked Quddús to come to her. When he did not comply with this request, Ṭáhirih herself came to the garden of Bahá'u'lláh without her veil, saying to them that the New Revelation had become manifest. At the sight of this woman, all the believers present were astonished and disturbed, as they realized the Proclamation of the Cause and the cancellation of some of the old laws. There was so much excitement about this unprecedented action that Bahá'u'lláh told one of the believers to read aloud the chapter of the Qur'án called Al-Qíyámat, about the Resurrection. In this it states that something astonishing would happen on the Promised Day. When the believers witnessed this happening they all fled away. Afterwards some did not object to it, and some others came again into the presence of Bahá'u'lláh to ask about this matter. Some say that when the matter of Badasht was referred to the Báb, He wrote telling the believers to follow Ṭáhirih's instructions, and spoke of her using the title Haḍrat-i Ṭáhirih. 'Abdu'l-Bahá uses this name instead of Qurratu'l-'Ayn in his book *Memorials of the Faithful.* Ḥájí Jání in his narrative speaks of Qurratu'l-'Ayn as the "Mother of the world."

The Conference in Badasht was in session only a short period. It is recorded that Bahá'u'lláh's sojourn there was twenty-two days. The exciting discussions attracted a number of inhabitants to the place and they soon plundered the Bábís, who did not resist or fight. Thus the Conference was broken up in disorder in this "Land of the Plain of Innovation," as Mírzá Jání had fancifully called Badasht at this time.

Until *The Dawn-Breakers* was published in 1932, one might well have wondered why the Bábu'l-Báb (Mullá Ḥusayn-i Bushrú'í) was not present at this Council; Chapter XVI makes it evident. He did not know about the Conference, and most of the believers gathered there were on their way to him in Mashhad. Also, in the narrative of Mírzá Jání, one finds a reason. The Bábu'l-Báb had intended to start from Mashhad for Mázindarán several days earlier than he actually did set out, for on the day of his intended departure from that city he visited the Shrine of Imám Riḍá in company with seventy of his followers.

A disturbance ending in riot took place between his followers and the townfolk, therefore Prince Ḥamzih Mírzá sent for the Bábu'l-Báb and detained him for a number of days in his, the prince's, camp. As soon as the Bábu'l-Báb was released, he gathered his party and started out. Just as he was near Bárfurúsh, news was received of the death of Muḥammad Sháh. This caused very disturbed conditions in the country and the Bábu'l-Báb and his followers—because they were believers in the Báb's Teachings—were attacked and ensnared at the Tomb of Shaykh Ṭabarsí. They could only defend themselves there; it was impossible for them to make their escape. They had not come there to make a fort, or to fight against the Muslims or the government, God forbid! They were hemmed in by a great beleaguering force, first composed of religious enemies and quickly strengthened by soldiers of the shah. Now as Quddús had sometime before this written a letter called the "Eternal Witness" in which he foretold the circumstances of his own and the Bábu'l-Báb's martyrdoms, the reader can understand what follows next in this narrative.

After the Conference in Badasht had been halted and the believers plundered and cruelly dispersed, while some were still at Niyálá en route, news came of the Bábu'l-Báb's calamity at the Ṭabarsí Tomb. Quddús had already reached his home in Bárfurúsh when he received the word. As soon as he could get away, he hurried to the Bábu'l-Báb and began to help organize the fort to be ready for the siege.[31] Fortunately for them this was possible, because in that moment most of the officials had gone down to Ṭihrán to the coronation of His Imperial Majesty Náṣiri'd-Dín Sháh on October 20, 1848. During this time, the men caught at Ṭabarsí made this place into what came to be known as Fort Ṭabarsí.

As soon as believers heard of the serious catastrophe which had befallen the Bábu'l-Báb and his followers, they set out even from the most distant provinces of Iran, and even from Iraq, to try to reach this fateful spot. They must have all known for a surety that in a little while every member of that devoted band at Fort Ṭabarsí would fall before the guns of the foe. What had the hastening Bábís seen in their visions? Or had they remembered the "Eternal Witness," the predic-

Historical Picture Service, Chicago

PERSIAN TRAVELERS

An artist's conception of Persian pilgrims on the way to Mas<u>sh</u>had

tion of coming death written by Quddus? Anyway, none of you, O readers, can doubt the loyalty and devotion of these followers, for what they suffered is almost beyond human endurance.

It is said that Ṭáhirih, when she heard of the Bábu'l-Báb's plight, determined to go in the disguise of a man into the fortress to help them. Bahá'u'lláh persuaded her not to do this. He said that first of all she could never succeed in entering, and moreover, war and strife are not desirable for anyone, above all for women; and besides this new Light had come to do away with war.

So one can see that even before Bahá'u'lláh declared His Mission He had laid down the principle against war. As soon as Bahá'u'lláh did proclaim His Cause,[32] He forbade the taking of revenge or killing to protect oneself, and such was the power of the Creative Word that from that time forward no Bahá'ís have ever killed others to save their own lives or to take revenge. The world cannot show a more wonderful record of submissiveness than the long list of Bahá'í martyrs reveals. The heroism, the sweetness, the gentleness, the joy with which the followers gave their lives is one of the great proofs that this Bahá'í Revelation is the Word of God to mankind in this universal cycle.

The Bábís in those first six years only knew the old way of self-defense; they had had so little opportunity to learn from the Báb. Yet they did glimpse the new Ideal, for they flung away their lives wholeheartedly, not for themselves but for the Cause. They had had no time to learn from the Báb, for He had been in prison and away from them all ever since His Declaration, except for those few short months in Iṣfahán. Who knows! Perhaps it all had to be like this. The Báb's task was to uproot the old order. Those early believers in the Báb's Teachings only by their never-to-be-forgotten martyrdoms could compel the sleeping, negligent world to become aware that again a Manifestation of God, a World Teacher, would come!

'Abdu'l-Bahá, in this same book, *Memorials of the Faithful,* says that Ṭáhirih was intercepted on her way to Ṭihrán from Bada<u>sh</u>t and that the captors sent her to the capital under the escort of certain low-class ruffians, and then later she was imprisoned in the house of Maḥmúd <u>Kh</u>án the Kalántar.³³

Ḥájí Mírzá Jání writes that Bahá'u'lláh, Mírzá Jání himself, and several others tried to reach Fort Ṭabarsí to bring relief. They had with them four thousand túmáns, about four thousand dollars, as well as goods and chattels. According to *The Dawn-Breakers,* in the beginning of December 1848 A.D. (Muḥarram 1265 A.H.), Bahá'u'lláh, faithful to the promise He had given to the Bábu'l-Báb, set out from Núr with a number of His friends to go to Fort Ṭabarsí. His intention was to reach that spot at night, allowing no halt in their journey; but His companions urged Him to seek a few hours' rest. Although He knew this delay would involve a great risk of being surprised by the enemy, He yielded to their earnest request and they were all captured. Another account reads that when they were within six miles of Ṭabarsí they were captured by the royalist officers, stripped, and taken to camp to be put to death. As Bahá'u'lláh belonged to such a noble, distinguished family of Mázindarán, certain of the royalist officers accorded Him their protection and sent Him on to Bárfurú<u>sh</u> where He suffered such afflictions as the pen is loath to portray. Two merchants of Ká<u>sh</u>án, the home city of Mírzá Jání, bought the latter's liberty with money. Friends in Ṭihrán had tried to dissuade Mírzá Jání from going to Ṭabarsí, but he had replied to them, "I shall suffer martyrdom in Ṭihrán Fort, and though on this journey I shall be taken captive I shall be released. Yet that I may have no cause for shame in not going, and that I may to the full accomplish my endeavor, I will go!''[34]

'Abdu'l-Bahá, in his account in *Memorials of the Faithful,* says that Bahá'u'lláh's intention was to go to Niyálá and thence to Fort Ṭabarsí; but the Governor of Ámul heard of this and came to Niyálá with seven hundred riflemen, surrounded Bahá'u'lláh and sent Him guarded by eleven mounted police to Ámul. While at Ámul, He was bastinadoed and then sent on to the capital.

I feel I cannot close the Bada<u>sh</u>t paragraphs without telling you of one more believer who was present at the Bada<u>sh</u>t Conference—this first Bahá'í Conference ever convened—Ḥájí Mullá Ismá'il of Qum, a divine of Karbilá who later in 1852, in Ṭihrán, was martyred. When he and the other Bábí prisoners were told to renounce their Faith or suffer death, he said to his companions, ''I, for my part, am resolved to confess my Faith and lay down my life; for if we fail to proclaim the advent of the Qá'im, who will proclaim it? And if we fail to direct men in the right way, to tear asunder the veils of heedlessness, to arouse them from the slumber of sloth, to demonstrate to them the worthlessness of this transitory world, and to give active testimony to the truth of this most high and ineffable Faith, who else will do so? Let every one, then, who is able to acquit himself of this obligation, come forth in all steadfastness and bear me company!'' Seven of these faithful lovers and loyal friends, according to the *Táríkh-i-Jadíd* gave themselves up to martyrdom in Ṭihrán. One of the group was Ḥájí Mírzá Siyyid 'Alí, the maternal Uncle of the Báb who had brought Him up from childhood and had always been one of His most loyal followers. The Seven Martyrs of Ṭihrán are historic, and perhaps some of the inspiration of this unsurpassed loyalty came from that gathering in Badas͟ht! So these believers who had gathered at Badas͟ht did *proclaim the Qá'im with their very lives!*

Quddús (Mullá Muḥammad-'Alí) had encouraged his men on New Year's Day, 1849, at Ṭabarsí, reciting to them after the bombardment: "We vouchsafe affliction to none until we have inscribed him among the saints. This affliction is the jewel of our treasure-house; we do not bestow jewels on everyone!"

Then those besiegers of the Fort Ṭabarsí, finding that they could not take it, finding they could not tear down the "Black Standards," the emblems of the faithful believers, nor withstand the attacks of those valiant souls who rode forth from the gate of the fort raising the cry of "Yá Ṣáḥibu'z-Zamán!" ("O Lord of the Age!") committed a base and treacherous act. Their leader promised the believers freedom and safe journey to their homes if they would surrender. He wrote upon the margin of a leaf of the sacred Qur'án his confirmation statement: "I swear by this most holy Book, by the righteousness of God who has revealed it, and the Mission of Him who was inspired by its Verses, that I cherish no other purpose than to promote peace and friendliness. Come forth from your stronghold and rest assured that no hand will be stretched forth against you."

Quddús received this Qur'án from the hands of the messenger; kissing it reverently he prayed and bade his men prepare to leave the fort. "By our response to their invitation," he said, "we shall enable them to demonstrate the sincerity of their intentions." *The Dawn-Breakers* gives a marvelous account of that exit. Quddús put on the green turban which the Báb had sent to him at the same time He sent the one to the Bábu'l-Báb, and the latter too had worn his on the day of his martyrdom. Two hundred and two believers went out together from that Shrine Ṭabarsí Fort. Of this number a few became separated from the larger group with Quddús, through a false report given by their enemies; thus this small number was made captive and later sold into slavery. It is from the words of these few men that we know about the historic siege of Fort Ṭabarsí. All the others were tortured and put to death.

Quddús, in his own home Bárfurúsh where they took him, suffered such atrocious cruelty that no pen can describe it. He was stripped of his clothes and his turban, which had been his gift from the Báb; was trampled in the mud; bare-headed, barefooted, and loaded with chains he was paraded through the streets, followed and scorned by the population, people who had known him from childhood and had seen the purity of his life. He was reviled and spit upon by the scum of the town, his body was pierced and mutilated by the howling mob. In the midst of these torments the voice of Quddús was heard in prayer: "Forgive O my God, the trespasses of this people. Deal with them in Thy mercy, for they know not what we have already discovered and cherish. I have striven to show them the path that leads to their salvation; behold how they have risen to overwhelm and kill me. Show them, O God, the way of Truth and turn their ignorance into faith!"

When the procession reached the public square, where the execution was to take place, Quddús, this youth of only twenty-seven years, cried out, "Would that my mother were with me, and could see with her own eyes the splendor of my nuptials!" As these words were being spoken the wild multitude fell upon him, tearing him limb from limb and throwing the scattered pieces into a fire which they had kindled for that purpose. Another account states that the Sa'ídu'l-'Ulamá had himself cut off Quddús' ears and struck him on the head with an axe.

The Bábu'l-Báb at the age of thirty-six years had met his heroic death a little earlier.

Let no one think that I speak of these frightful crimes in order to criticize the fanatical Muslims who perpetrated them in the name of God. No! I understand that they belonged to the old epoch; likewise I do not forget that great atrocities have been committed in our Western world in the name of religion. I mention these historical incidents because they prove with what travail the Word of God is brought into the world from age to age. Shall we never learn from the past religious cycles to *investigate truth* before we kill the Prophets and their first followers?

So let us leave Fort Ṭabarsí, but as we are turning away, we take this last glimpse: the conquerors are looting the dead victims, and from the pocket of one brave young martyr they are drawing out . . . what? A little roasted horseflesh which had become too hard for him to eat! Surely hearts are moved at the courage and the sufferings of these first followers of the pure and holy Báb!

CHAPTER III

ṬÁHIRIH'S MARTYRDOM AND THE AFTERMATH

NOW I SHALL present to you all that I have been able to learn about Ṭáhirih's communication with His Imperial Majesty Náṣiri'd-Dín Sháh. When she was brought into his presence, after her return from Badasht, on seeing her he said, "I like her looks: leave her, and let her be." It is related that His Imperial Majesty sent her a letter to the kalántar's house, the gist of which was that he urged her to deny the Báb and again become a true Muslim. If she would do this, then he would give her an exalted position as the guardian of the ladies of his household: he would make her his bride. She wrote a reply in verse on the back of his letter and had it returned to the sháhansháh. The English translation, which cannot do justice to the beauty of the original poem, is about as follows:

Kingdom, wealth and ruling be for thee.
Wandering, becoming a poor dervish and calamity be for me.
If that station is good, let it be for thee.
And if this station is bad, I long for it; let it be for me!

After the shah read this, he commented on her wonderful spirit and her courage. His words were: "So far history has not shown such a woman to us."

The relative of Ṭáhirih in Qazvín told me that the day before her martyrdom she was called to the presence of His Imperial Majesty Náṣiri'd-Dín Sháh. He said to her that day,

"Why should you be a believer in the Báb?" She replied not with her own words, but from the Qur'án which was about as follows:

> I worship not that which ye worship,
> And ye do not worship that which I worship;
> I shall never worship that which ye worship,
> Neither will ye worship that which I worship.
> To you be your religion; to me my religion.[35]

His Majesty bent his head in silence for some time and then arose and left the room without saying anything. However, I heard that the eunuch and others around the shah were determined she should be killed, and the next day they had her murdered without the shah's knowledge; and he was very grieved when he learned of it.

During her imprisonment in the kalántar's house she was kept first in a little room outside where there were no stairs; a ladder had to be put up each time she wished to descend. One of the princesses who was a poet came and walked past this little house, hoping to see Ṭáhirih. She did see her and later in one of her books this princess tells how radiantly happy Ṭáhirih was. Everywhere, in every history, and all who have spoken of her, tell of her joy in her religion. She was always bright and enthusiastic and even when in greatest danger herself, she was ever inspiring others with courage. She was not only a martyr, but she was a smiling, joyful young woman. I say young woman, for she was only about thirty-two years old, or at most thirty-six years old, when she was put to death in August 1852.

There have been different accounts of her death, and they differ as to how the deed was done, but one and all agree that she knew beforehand, through insight, that she had to die and that she met her murder with unsurpassed bravery.

NÁṢIRI'D-DÍN SHÁH

First, I quote what 'Abdu'l-Bahá said of her and of her death. Once He wrote, "Among the women of our time is Ṭáhirih, the daughter of a Muslim priest. At the time of the appearance of the Báb, she showed such tremendous courage and power, that all who heard her were astonished. She threw aside her veil, despite the immemorial custom of the Persians; and, although it was considered impolite to speak with men, this heroic woman carried on conversations with the most learned men, and in every meeting she vanquished them. When imprisoned she said: 'You can kill me as soon as you like, but you cannot stop the emancipation of women!' "

He says of Ṭáhirih in His *Memorials of the Faithful* that she was imprisoned in the kalántar's home.[36] Once there was a great festivity in this home. It was the betrothal of the kalántar's son. Many ladies of the aristocracy were present, princesses, wives of ministers and other notables. It was a brilliant and distinguished gathering. Music and dancing were features and everyone was merry. Jináb-i Ṭáhirih entered and soon began conversing about the Teaching of the Báb; all were so interested and impressed that they left the dancers to gather about her and to hear her inspired word. They almost forgot about the betrothal entertainment.

Thus she lived in the house of the kalántar until a certain foolish and ignorant Bábí—and some historians say that he had two or three accomplices—crazed by the martyrdom of his Beloved, committed the crime of trying to kill the shah on August 15, 1852. The shah was not hurt and was able to hold his usual reception the next day, but this Bábí's horrible deed has blackened the pages of Bábí history throughout the civilized world.

On the other hand, never in the history of nations has such a punishment been meted out to innocent people as Náṣiri'd-Dín Shah and his government hurled upon all the believers in the Báb. Though they had known nothing of this plot, they were searched out and on September 15, 1852, nearly eighty were put to death in the most fiendish ways that could be devised. The shah, the prime minister, the chief of the farrá<u>sh</u>es,[37] the whole government, became so alarmed and wrought up in their hatred that it reacted upon themselves. They became afraid and therefore they decreed that each class of society should share in the bloodshed, and each be made responsible for the execution of one or more of these believers. The Machiavellian cruelty of each class would be an indication of its loyalty to the shah. This account has only to do with the martyrdom of Ṭáhirih, and to tell you what happened to Bahá'u'lláh, but the others you can read about in *The Dawn-Breakers, A Traveller's Narrative,* and in *Tárí<u>kh</u>-i-Jadíd.*

The day after the attempt on the shah's life, Bahá'u'lláh rode forth into Niyávarán, which was the abode of the Royal Court and the headquarters of the Imperial Army. He was arrested and brought in chains to Ṭihrán. I saw the underground prison where they had placed Him (but now this loathsome hole has been made over into a tobacco place). I saw the court where they took Him, put His feet into stocks, and gave Him fifteen lashes. He had done nothing; none of them had. They were innocent and were just as shocked at this terrible crime as was the government itself. There might have been no deliverance from death for Bahá'u'lláh had not His Majesty ordered His particular case investigated and examined by the ministers of the Imperial Court. His innocence was fully established. Therefore He was not killed, but His confiscated estates were not returned to Him, neither was He set free, but four months later He was exiled to Bag<u>h</u>dád. Perhaps because of His high station in Ṭihrán, He escaped death, but we who are Bahá'ís know that He continued to live because it was God's Will for the establishment of this universal cycle.

Efforts were made by some of the European representatives at the Iranian Court to induce the shah to execute the condemned without subjecting them to tortures, which there was every reason to believe would be superadded to the death penalty. These efforts, however, were fruitless.

Ṭáhirih, living as a prisoner in the kalántar's house, certainly had had no part in this attempt on the shah's life; yet because she was a believer in the Báb's Teachings, she was doomed. Officials came, according to the *Memorials of the Faithful,* and took her from the kalántar's home on the pretext that she was to be conducted to the house of the prime minister. She had, that morning, carefully bathed, and perfumed herself with rose water, dressed herself in her best white gown, said good-bye to everybody in the house, announcing to them that in the evening she was going on a long journey. Her prophetic soul had made her aware. She was ready and went with them when they came for her that night. They took her to a garden. The executioners hesitated for a while to carry out the order issued for her death and even refused to do it. Then they found a Negro slave who was drunk; he put a handkerchief into Ṭáhirih's mouth and strangled her. Afterwards, they threw her down into a well in the garden, and threw stones and rubbish on her. "But to the last moment of her life," said 'Abdu'l-Bahá, "Her Highness Ṭáhirih was joyous and happy, and was looking forward to the Bounties of the Abhá Kingdom. In this manner she sacrificed her precious life. May her soul be happy and joyful in the Abhá Kingdom!"

There is a difference of opinion about the way she was put to death. Dr. Jakob Polak, an Austrian, formerly physician of the shah of Iran and professor in the Medical College of Ṭihrán, wrote a book in 1865, *Persien Das Land und Seine Bewohner,* in which he said he witnessed Ṭáhirih's execution and that she endured her lingering death with "superhuman fortitude."

M. le Comte de Gobineau of Paris, in his book *Les religions et les philosophies dans l'Asie Centrale,* published in 1865, states that Ṭáhirih was burned, but that the executioners first strangled her. Another account says she was strangled with a bowstring. They tried to force her to take off her veil; she would not, and they drew the bowstring around her throat over the veil and thus strangled her. Then they threw her, while she was still living, into a dry well and filled it up with earth and stones.

While I was in Ṭihrán in the year 1930, Dr. Susan I. Moody gave me an account of Ṭáhirih's martyrdom that had been given to her by Jináb-i Adíb, an old and famous Bahá'í teacher who had visited Bahá'u'lláh in 'Akká. Formerly Jináb-i Adíb had been a university professor and later he founded the Ṭarbíyat School for boys in Ṭihrán. His father had been a teacher in the family of Fatḥ-'Alí Sháh. The following is written under the signature of Jináb-i Adíb, and he states he was an intimate friend of Qulí who came with Ṭáhirih to Ṭihrán. I only quote the part about Ṭáhirih's martyrdom:

"In every meeting held in Ṭihrán, both women and men were speaking in Ṭáhirih's praise and honor. Many high-born, loving women came to her and were filled with joy because of her hopeful words. All were attracted by her eloquence, and people of all classes, even the royalty and ministers of state, on entering her presence humbly bowed before her. Her speeches and explanations were spread all over Iran, and no one had the least doubt about her erudition and immense knowledge.

"While a youth I used to study philosophy with Mírzá 'Abdu'l-Vahháb, a brother of Ṭáhirih. When I had any doubts or made errors, I used to ask his help. One day in summer I went to him in the courtyard of his house. He was alone and as it was a hot day he wore a loose, light garment. After sitting a little and finding a good opportunity, I said, 'I wanted to ask you some questions but I have hesitated; now if you will permit me, I shall ask you.' He gave permission and I continued, 'Both the learning and the perfection of Ṭáhirih are so spread among the people that minds are amazed. No one knows better than you and I want to know from you the truth or falsity of this matter.'

"Then he sighed and responded, 'You have only heard word of Ṭáhirih; alas, you have not seen her! Know verily, that in a meeting where she sat neither I nor anyone else could say a word. It was as if all the former and future books were with her. She used to explain a subject by bringing forth demonstrations and proofs from the learned books, page by page, so that no one had the power to deny. Ḥájí Mullá Taqí, who was assassinated, was heard to say many times, "When the signs of the promised One appear, the Zindíq[38] of Qazvín will also appear, and the words of the Zindíq will be the words of a woman's religion! Now this woman and her religion have appeared." In fact her talks and explanations were the true witnesses for her. Since then, the clergy have prevented all women from studying lest they should become believers like Ṭáhirih.'

"About this time, in 1852, some fanatical Bábís fired shots at Náṣiri'd-Dín Sh̲áh and all the people believing in the Báb's Teachings were in danger. . . . Maḥmúd Kh̲án, the kalántar, informed the shah and the Grand Vazír that Ṭáhirih was in his house, but they feared to sentence her to death without a trial, knowing that she was intimate with and

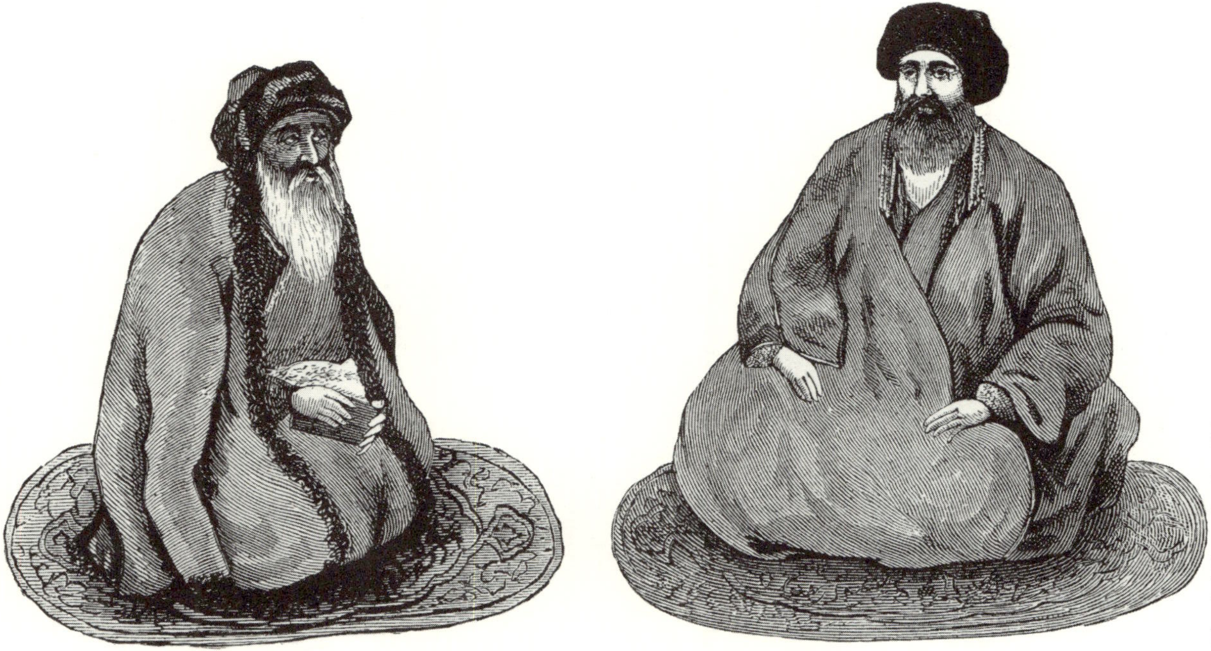

Historical Picture Service, Chicago

A MULLÁ (Muslim priest, left) AND A SIYYID
(descendant of Muḥammad, right)

sincerely loved by the most honorable women of high degree, who would raise a clamor which no one could suppress.

"Let me relate one incident to show her influence: two ladies who were acquainted with the family of the kalántar have told me that, during her imprisonment in his house, the kalántar made preparations for the betrothal of his son. These festivities last several days and invitations are given out day by day to people of various degrees of social standing. During all this preparation and merry-making, Ṭáhirih ceased not from delivering her message, and so eloquently that the people deserted their days of pleasure. They were so filled with wonder and dazed by her explanations and eloquence that all sources of pleasure provided for their enjoyment were forgotten and forsaken. They were as if enchanted by her talks and actions, and were seeking to know why she had become an infidel (for so she seemed to them).

"Wishing to accomplish her downfall, the chiefs of the government commanded Ḥájí Mullá Kaní and Ḥájí Mullá Muḥammad Andirmání, two of the most learned and famous clergymen of Ṭihrán, to interrogate her, and declared that whatever these two Muslim divines decided upon should be done.[39] Accordingly, discussions were held in the home of Maḥmúd K͟hán, the kalántar. In every meeting she debated with them and they were defeated. Still they remained unconvinced and finally wrote a sentence as follows: 'This woman is astray and a leader astray of others; therefore, her death is necessary and expedient.' The government accepted this, added some false charges to it and spread it broadcast among men and women. Thus all were anticipating her death. However, notwithstanding the proclamation, through fear they killed her secretly by night.

"As this mortal one [Jináb-i Adíb] sleeping or waking was greedily searching to discover the truth of the Bahá'í

Cause, which at this time was not clear to me, I desired to investigate for myself. Accordingly, I went to one of the relatives who was intimate and confidential with me, a man older than myself, a mullá and inclined toward the sect of the Ṣúfís, and I asked him, 'What do you know about this occurrence?' He replied, 'I have no exact information, but it is easy to obtain it, for the eldest son of the kalántar, who is my intimate friend, belongs to the Ṣúfís. On a certain day I shall invite him to be my guest; you will also be present and we can question him.'

"Meeting together on the day appointed, I said, 'I have heard various versions of the facts concerning the fate of Ṭáhirih, but since Her Highness was imprisoned in your home, you certainly know better than any one else all the circumstances.' He replied, 'On the day that she was secretly assassinated by night, like one who had been informed beforehand, she bathed and changed all of her clothing and came downstairs. One by one she asked pardon of the household for having troubled them. She was like a traveler, with the utmost pleasure and joy taking leave before starting on a journey. Near sunset, according to her usual habit, she was slowly walking to and fro on the upper veranda. She conversed with no one, but was secretly whispering to herself. This continued until three hours after sunset. A strict command had been given that on that night, no one should leave his apartment, otherwise he would be punished.

" 'My father came to me and said, "I have attended to all necessary precautions and have commanded that the watchmen be very alert at the crossroads lest there might arise some disturbance. Now I want you, with the utmost caution, to take this woman with the servants to the garden of Ílkhání and deliver her to Sardár-i Kull, 'Azíz Khán, and you must stay there until the case is settled. Then come back and report to me, so that I may go and inform the shah.'' After that he arose and told me to come with him, and we went upstairs together. As we reached the door of the upper room, we saw that she was ready. My father said to her: ''Let us start immediately; you must go to another place.'' Without hesitating, she came. As we reached the outer door, we found my father's own horse ready; she mounted and my father put on her his own cloak so that no one should recognize the rider as a woman. Then with a large guard of bold servants we started, going in a roundabout way until we reached the garden, where she was dismounted and was put into a servant's room on the ground floor.

'' 'I went upstairs and entered the presence of the sardár who was alone and awaiting us. I gave him my father's salutations and message. He asked, ''No one recognized you on the way?'' I replied, ''No one.'' He then called in a servant, greeted him in a friendly way, inquiring about his health, and then said, ''Have you received a gift for any of your people on this journey?'' He said no. Then the sardár presented him with a handful of one túmán gold pieces, saying, ''Well, take this now and send it to them, and later I shall compensate you.'' Then he added, ''Take this silk handkerchief and go and twist it around the neck of this Bábí woman and choke her, for she is the cause of leading the people astray.'' The servant left the room and I accompanied him. He went ahead and I stood at the door. When he approached Ṭáhirih, she looked at him and uttered some words. Suddenly I saw him coming back, hanging his head and talking softly to himself in Turkish as he went out of the door. I returned to the sardár and explained the whole proceeding.

'' 'He called for coffee. After reflecting for a while, he asked for his butler and said, ''I once dismissed a servant who used to do evil things. Where is he?'' The butler replied that this servant was now serving in the kitchen. The sardár said, "Tell him to come here." Shortly after, a dirty man with a very evil countenance came in. The master said to him, "Do you not see into what a condition you have fallen? If you repent and stop your evil deeds, I will restore you to your former position, and you may spend your time in pleasure." The man answered, "Hereafter I will never disobey you." His master said, "Very well. I am sure you have not taken anything to drink [literal translation: serpent's poison]. Go to the other room and take a cup full, then return, and I will give your tools and clothing." He went and returned. The sardár said, "You are such a brave man, can you strangle the woman who is downstairs?" He said yes, and went out and I went with him.

" 'As soon as he reached her, he quickly wrapped the thing around her throat so tightly that she became unconscious and fell down. He kicked her in the side and chest. A farrásh came, and they carried her in her own garments and threw her into a well which was at the lower end of the garden, afterwards filling up the well with stones and dirt. I returned home and gave my father a full account of this affair.' "[40]

The Dawn-Breakers also speaks of the kalántar's son and that he accompanied Ṭáhirih to the garden where she was put to death. I quote a few passages: "Her stay in Ṭihrán was marked by many proofs of the warm affection and high esteem in which she was held by the leading women of the capital. She had reached, indeed, in those days the high-water mark of her popularity. The house where she was confined was besieged by her women admirers, who thronged her doors, eager to enter her presence and to seek the benefit of her knowledge. Among these ladies, the wife of Kalántar distinguished herself by the extreme reverence she showed to

Ṭáhirih. Acting as her hostess, she introduced into her presence the flower of womanhood in Ṭihrán, served her with extraordinary enthusiasm, and never failed to contribute her share in deepening her influence among her womenfolk. Persons with whom the wife of the kalántar was intimately connected have heard her relate the following: 'One night, whilst Ṭáhirih was staying in my home, I was summoned to her presence and found her fully adorned, dressed in a gown of snow-white silk. Her room was redolent with the choicest perfume. I expressed to her my surprise at so unusual a sight. "I am preparing to meet my Beloved," she said, "and wish to free you from the cares and anxieties of my imprisonment." I was much startled at first, and wept at the thought of separation from her. "Weep not," she sought to reassure me. "The time of your lamentation is not yet come. I wish to share with you my last wishes, for the hour when I shall be arrested and condemned to suffer martyrdom is fast approaching. I would request you to allow your son to accompany me to the scene of my death and to ensure that the guards and executioner into whose hands I shall be delivered will not compel me to divest myself of this attire. It is also my wish that my body be thrown into a pit, and that that pit be filled with earth and stones. Three days after my death a woman will come and visit you, to whom you will give this package which I now deliver into your hands. My last request is that you permit no one henceforth to enter my chamber. From now until the time when I shall be summoned to leave this house, let no one be allowed to disturb my devotions. This day I intend to fast—a fast which I shall not break until I am brought face to face with my Beloved." . . . That day and night, I several times, unable to contain myself, arose and stole away to the threshold of that room and stood silently at her door, eager to listen to whatever might be falling from her lips. I was enchanted by the melody of that voice which intoned the praise of her Beloved. Four hours after sunset, I heard a knocking at the door. I hastened immediately to my son, and acquainted him with the wishes of Ṭáhirih. He pledged his word that he would fulfill every instruction she had given me. . . . My son, who opened the door, informed me that the farrás̲h̲es of 'Azíz K̲h̲án-i Sardár were standing at the gate, demanding that Ṭáhirih be immediately delivered into their hands. I was struck with terror by the news, and, as I tottered to her door and with trembling hands unlocked it, found her veiled and prepared to leave her apartment. She was pacing the floor when I entered, and was chanting a litany expressive of both grief and triumph. . . . She placed in my hand the key to her chest, in which she said she had left for me a few trivial things as a remembrance of her stay in my house. "Whenever you open this chest," she said, "and behold the things it contains, you will, I hope, remember me and rejoice in my gladness."

'With these words she bade me her last farewell, and, accompanied by my son, disappeared from before my eyes. . . .

'Three hours later my son returned, his face drenched with tears, hurling imprecations at the Sardár and his abject lieutenants.'

"May future generations be enabled to present a worthy account of a life which her contemporaries have failed adequately to recognize. May future historians perceive the full measure of her influence, and record the unique services this great woman has rendered to her land and its people. May the followers of the Faith which she served so well strive to follow her example, recount her deeds, collect her writings, unfold the secret of her talents, and establish her, for all time, in the memory and affections of the peoples and kindreds of the earth."[41]

We are grateful to the Oriental scholars who have

written about her great life. There resided in Ṭihrán, in the years 1855–1858, a French diplomat, le Comte de Gobineau, a brilliant writer who studied the Bábí Movement. He has written about Ṭáhirih in his classic book, *Les religions et les philosophies dans l'Asie Centrale.*

Lord Curzon, in his book, *Persia and the Persian Question,* states: "Beauty and the female sex also lent their consecration to the new creed, and the heroism of the lovely but ill-fated poetess of Qazvín, Zarrín-Táj (Crown of Gold) or Qurratu'l-'Ayn (Solace of the Eyes), who, throwing off the veil, carried the missionary torch far and wide, is one of the most affecting episodes in modern history."[42]

Valentine Chirol, in *The Middle Eastern Question,* comments: "No memory is more deeply venerated or kindles greater enthusiasm than hers [Ṭáhirih's], and the influence which she wielded in her lifetime still inures to her sex."[43]

Sir Francis Younghusband, in his book *The Gleam* comments: "Almost the most remarkable figure in the whole movement was the poetess, Qurratu'l-'Ayn. She was known for her virtue, piety and learning, and had been finally converted on reading some of the verses and exhortations of the Báb. So strong in her faith did she become that although she was both rich and noble she gave up wealth, child, name and position for her Master's service and set herself to proclaim and establish His doctrine. The beauty of her speech was such as to draw guests from a marriage feast rather than listen to the music provided by the host."[44]

Dr. T. K. Cheyne, in his book, *The Reconciliation of Races and Religions,* also pays tribute: "The harvest sown in Islamic lands by Qurratu'l-'Ayn is now beginning to appear. A letter addressed to the 'Christian Commonwealth' last June informs us that forty Turkish suffragettes are being deported from Constantinople to 'Akká (so long the prison of

Bahá'u'lláh): 'During the last few years suffrage ideas have been spreading quietly behind in the harems. The men were ignorant of it; everybody was ignorant of it; and now suddenly the floodgate is opened and the men of Constantinople have thought it necessary to resort to drastic measures. Suffrage clubs have been organized, intelligent memorials incorporating the women's demands have been drafted and circulated; women's journals and magazines have sprung up, publishing excellent articles; and public meetings were held. Then one day the members of these clubs—four hundred of them—cast away their veils. The staid, fossilised class of society were shocked, the good Musulmans were alarmed, and the Government forced into action. These four hundred liberty-loving women were divided into several groups. One group composed of forty have been exiled to 'Akká, and will arrive in a few days. Everybody is talking about it and it is really surprising to see how numerous are those in favor of removing the veils from the faces of the women. Many men with whom I have talked think the custom not only archaic, but thought-stifling. The Turkish authorities, thinking to extinguish this light of liberty, have greatly added to its flame. . . .''[45]

This much I have learned from many sources, some from published works, some from manuscripts, much by word of mouth from the friends and relatives of Ṭáhirih.

However, before I went to Iran, I had seen the influence of Ṭáhirih in all the five continents I had visited. As I stood beside the well in a little garden in the heart of Ṭihrán where her dear body was cast, I thought of the lines in the beautiful drama, ''God's Heroes,'' written by Mrs. Laura Dreyfus-Barney of Paris, in which she has told the story of this great Eastern sister so marvelously:

''Cease your profanations! Weak of purpose! Do you

think you can bury her there? She will reappear, and be ever before you all! You have rendered her immortal in the minds of men and her spirit of love will be transmitted to millions of living hearts. You have undone your work and have established her fame. Forever after Ṭáhirih will inspire courage and sincerity and truth!"

And I agree with Sulaymán Názim Big, the great author and poet of Turkey, who said in his book *Náṣiri'd-Dín S͟háh and the Bábís:* "O Ṭáhirih, you are worth a thousand Náṣiri-d-Dín S͟háhs!"

Traveling throughout the world, I find that they know about Ṭahirih everywhere. Mrs. Marianna Hainisch of Vienna, Austria, mother of the President of Austria, when I visited her in 1925, said to me, "The greatest ideal of womanhood all my life has been Ṭáhirih [Qurratu'l-'Ayn] of Qazvín, Iran. I was only seventeen years old when I heard of her life and her martyrdom, but I said, 'I shall try to do for the women of Austria what Ṭáhirih gave her life to do for women of Persia.' " No woman in Austria has done so much for freedom and education for women as has Mrs. Hainisch.

Mrs. Hainisch's most loved friend was Miss Marie von Najmajer, and Miss von Najmajer wrote a great epic poem, "Qurratu'l-'Ayn," which is one of the charming classics in the German language.

Professor G. Weil, of the Staatsbibliothek of Berlin, which is considered to be one of the three greatest libraries in the world, asked me for the loan of "God's Heroes," the story of Ṭáhirih. The next day when he returned it he said, "I am delighted with this beautiful book, we shall order it today. We wish to buy every book we can get on the Bahá'í Faith."

Students from Iran, studying in Berlin and in Paris, have said to me that at home, fathers who wish their daughters to progress, often say to them: "Be a Ṭáhirih! Be a Qurratu'l-'Ayn!"

One great Iranian prince at the League of Nations in 1927, said to me, "I was only a young man when I heard of the martyrdom of the gifted poetess Ṭáhirih [Qurratu'l-'Ayn] in Ṭihrán, and I tell you I wept for three days."

The late Arminius Vambéry of Budapest, Hungary, in his book, *Meine Wanderungen und Erlebnisse in Persien (My Migrations and What I Saw in Persia in 1867),* speaks of the Báb and His followers. Later, in 1913, he met 'Abdu'l-Bahá when the latter visited Budapest, and he became a Bahá'í. His grandson, George Vambéry, a youth twenty years old when I visited Budapest in 1926, was greatly interested in the study of Ṭáhirih's life.

Nawab Sir Amin Jung Bahadur, Minister-in-Waiting upon His Exalted Highness the great Nizam of Hyderabad, Deccan, India, is a Muslim, but he has read much about the Bahá'í Faith. When I was invited to his fine library which he calls his "Treasury," he said to me, in June 1930, that what had attracted him most to this Bahá'í religion was the wonderful life of Ṭáhirih. He wished so much to obtain her poems in the Persian language.

Mrs. Sarojina Naidu, also of Hyderabad, Deccan, who is India's best known woman, and most eloquent woman speaker, a poet whose works are translated into many languages, the greatest worker for women in India so far in this century, had also said to me on June 4, 1930, when I traveled again through India to promote the Teachings of Bahá'u'lláh, "Oh, for ten years I have longed to have the poems of Ṭáhirih!" So, as a Bahá'í friend in Iran had copied some of Ṭáhirih's poems and placed them in a lovely little book for a gift to me, I was trying to get some of these copied in longhand for her, and for some other scholars in India, including the celebrated Islamic writer and poet, Sir Muhammad Iqbal of Lahore.

Knowing this, Mr. Isfandiyár K. B. Bak̲h̲tiyárí, a most devoted Persian Bahá'í of Karachi, India, who was with me that day in Lahore, took my gift and had a thousand little Persian books printed so that they might be given out in India. Ṭáhirih was a great poet, but as most of her poems were spiritual and were about the Báb and His Holy Cause, they were burned with her other writings. Some of her poems are set to music and I often heard the records on the victrolas in Persian homes.

O Ṭáhirih! you have not passed away, you have only passed on. Your spiritual, courageous individuality will forever inspire, ennoble, and refine humanity; your songs of the spirit will be treasured in innumerable hearts. You are to this day our thrilling, living Bahá'í teacher. And your work is only beginning, for you will bring our Bahá'í Faith to many millions yet unborn.

Audio-Visual Department, Bahá'í World Center

MARTHA ROOT

EPILOGUE

HAVING BROUGHT this short narrative to a close, I wish, in epilogue, to quote the words of Shoghi Effendi, the Guardian of the Bahá'í Faith, in his book, *The Dawn-Breakers,* that they may ever be our on-going:

"And yet who knows what achievements, greater than any that the past and the present have witnessed, may not still be in store for those into whose hands so precious a heritage [as the Bahá'í Faith] has been entrusted? Who knows but that out of the turmoil which agitates the face of present-day society there may not emerge, sooner than we expect, the World Order of Bahá'u'lláh, the bare outline of which is being but faintly discerned among the world-wide communities that bear His name? For, great and marvelous as have been the achievements of the past, the glory of the golden age of the Cause, whose promise lies embedded within the shell of Bahá'u'lláh's immortal utterance, is yet to be revealed. Fierce as may seem the onslaught of the forces of darkness that may still afflict this Cause, desperate and prolonged as may be that struggle, . . . the ascendancy it will eventually obtain will be such as no other Faith has ever in its history achieved. The welding of the communities of East and West into a world-wide Brotherhood of which poets and dreamers have sung, and the promise of which lies at the very core of the Revelation conceived by Bahá'u'lláh; the recognition of His Law as the indissoluble bond uniting the peoples and nations of the earth; and the proclamation of the reign of the Most Great Peace, are but a few among the chapters of the glorious tale which the consummation of the Faith of Bahá'u'lláh will unfold.

"Who knows but that triumphs unsurpassed in splendor are not in store for the mass of Bahá'u'lláh's toiling followers? Surely, we stand too near the colossal edifice His hand has reared to be able, at the present stage of the evolution of His Revelation, to claim to be able even to conceive the full measure of its promised glory. Its past history, stained by the blood of countless martyrs, may well inspire us with the thought that, whatever may yet befall this Cause, however formidable the forces that may still assail it, however numerous the reverses it will inevitably suffer, its onward march can never be stayed, and that it will continue to advance until the very last promise, enshrined within the words of Bahá'u'lláh, shall have been completely redeemed."[46]

APPENDIX I

ṬÁHIRIH'S POEMS

CONCERNING THE POEMS of Ṭáhirih, Professor Edward G. Browne of Cambridge University, in the *Journal of the Royal Asiatic Society* (Vol. XXI, p. 934), has written the following most illuminating comment: "Turning from the Báb, there is another figure amongst those who took part in this sad drama which irresistibly commands our attention. I mean the beautiful and accomplished Qurratu'l-'Ayn, the heroine, poetess, of the new Faith, distinguished by the title of 'Jináb-i-Ṭáhirih,' 'Her Excellence the Pure.' Anxious as I was to obtain some of her poems, I only met with a very limited amount of success. None of the Bábís at Shíráz whom I conversed with had any in their possession, and they said that Qazvín and Hamadán, where Qurratu'l-'Ayn had preached, and Ṭihrán, where she had suffered martyrdom, would be the most likely places to obtain them. However, at Yazd I saw copies of two short poems (ghazals) attributed to her authorship. . . .

"Although these poems, especially the first, can only be referred very doubtfully to the authorship of Qurratu'l-'Ayn, it must be borne in mind that the odium which attaches to the name of the Bábí amongst Iranian Muḥammadans would render impossible the recitation by them of verses confessedly composed by her. If therefore, she were actually the authoress of poems, the grace and beauty of which compelled an involuntary admiration even from her enemies, it would seem extremely probable that they should seek to justify their right to admire them by attributing them to some other writer, and this view is supported by an assertion which I have heard made by a learned Persian with whom I was acquainted in Ṭihrán, and who, though not actually a Bábí, did not lack a certain amount of sympathy for those who were such, to the effect that many poems written by Qurratu'l-'Ayn were amongst the favorite songs of the people, who were for the most part unaware of their authorship. Open allusion to the Báb had of course been cut out or altered, so that no one could tell the source from whence they came.

"Without pretending to assert positively that either of these two poems is by Qurratu'l-'Ayn, I venture to give a translation of the second of them which I have attempted to versify in imitation of the original metre, so as to afford a better idea of its style than could be given by a literal rendering in prose. In this I have endeavoured to adhere as closely as possible to the sense of the original, even though the English may have suffered thereby.

"This second poem is:

The thralls of yearning love constrain in the bonds of pain and calamity
These broken-hearted lovers of thine to yield their lives in their zeal for thee.
Though with sword in hand my Darling stand with intent to slay, though I sinless be,
If it pleases him this tyrant's whim, I am well content with his tyranny.
As in sleep I lay at the break of day that cruel Charmer came to me,
And in the grace of his form and face the dawn of the Morn I seemed to see;

The musk of Cathay might perfume gain from the scent those fragrant tresses rain,
While his eyes demolish a faith in vain attacked by the pagans of Tartary.
With you who condemn both love and wine for the hermit's cell and the zealot's shrine,
What can I do? for our Faith divine you hold a thing of infamy?
The tangled curls of thy darling's hair, and thy saddle and steed are thy only care.
In thy heart the Absolute hath no share, nor the thought of the poor man's poverty.
Sikandar's pomp and display be thine, the Kalántar's habit and way be mine,
That, if it please thee, I resign, while this, though bad, is enough for me,
The country of 'I' and 'we' forsake; thy home in Annihilation make,
Since fearing not this step to take, thou shalt gain the highest felicity."

Another poem of Ṭáhirih's which Professor Edward G. Browne published in his book, *A Traveller's Narrative,* (English edition, Cambridge University Press, P. 315) is:

The effulgence of thy face flashed forth and the rays of thy visage arose on high;
Why lags the word 'Am I not your Lord?'* 'Yea that thou art' let us make reply.

*Why do you hesitate to lay claim to a divine nature? Were you to do so, all of us would admit your claim.

'Am I not's' appeal from thy drum to greet what 'Yeas'
do the drums of devotion beat;
At the gates of my heart I behold the feet and the tents
of the host of calamity.

The following poems of Ṭáhirih in Persian were given to me with a few others, when I was leaving Iran after a four months' Bahá'í teaching tour in 1930. I came direct to India in May of that year, and immediately in traveling through India I found that the cultured classes know about Qurratu'l-'Ayn and were deeply interested in her poems. I asked my good friend, Mr. Isfandiyar K. B. Bak͟htiyarí, a most devoted Iranian Bahá'í residing in Karachi, if he could please copy for me, in longhand, a few of these poems to give to some poets and other writers in India.

At once, this great Bahá'í had a thousand copies printed in Karachi and these were given out during the memorable tour through India and Burma in 1930. Then again in 1933, in memory of that same visit, Mr. Bak͟htiyarí printed a second edition of one thousand copies which have been given to the literati of India. It is astonishing how many of the educated classes in India know the Persian language, and they know the life and poems of Qurratu'l-'Ayn better than we in the West know them.

I have asked Mr. Bak͟htiyarí please to take from the little book seven of these Persian poems written by Ṭáhirih, and I include them in this supplement. Some day all these will be translated into the English language and into many other tongues.

Many Indian scholars know Ṭáhirih's poems by heart. One of the leading Indian Orientalists, Professor M. Hidayat Hosain, Fellow of the Royal Asiatic Society, of Bengal, now Philological Secretary of the Royal Asiatic Society, Calcutta, is one of these.* The whole five continents have scholars who write asking to know more about Ṭáhirih, her life and her poetry "touched by the Flame of God."

*Professor Hosain has written a most interesting article entitled, "A Female Martyr of the Bábí Faith" published in a book called *Proceedings of the Idara-i-Maarif-i-Islamia,* a convention held in Lahore in 1933, and the volume is dedicated to the Nizam of Hyderabad, Deccan.

اشعار گوهر بار حضرت طاهره
(قرة العين)

گر بتو افتدم نظر چهره بچهره روبرو
شرح دهم غم تورا نکته بنکته مو بمو
از پی دیدن رخت همچو صبا فتاده ام
خانه بخانه در بدر کوچه بکوچه کو بکو
میرود از فراق تو خون دل از دو دیده ام
دجله بدجله یم بیم چشمه بچشمه جو بجو
دور دهان تنگ تو عارض عنبرین خطت
غنچه بغنچه گل بگل لاله بلاله بو ببو
ابرو و چشم و خال تو صید نموده مرغ دل
طبع بطبع و دل بدل مهر بمهر و خو بخو
مهر ترا دل حزین بافته بر قماش جان
رشته برشته نخ بنخ تار بتار و پو بپو
در دل خویش طاهره گشت و ندید جز تورا
صفحه بصفحه لا بلا پرده بپرده تو بتو

و من ابیاتها الحسنة روح الله روحها

هله ای گروه عمائیان بکشید هلهله ولا
که ظهور دلبر ماعیان شده فاش و ظاهر و برملا
بز نید نغمه زهر طرف که ز وجه طلعت ما عرف
رفع القناع و قد کشف ظلم اللیال قد انجلی
برسید با سپه طرب صنمی عجم صمدی عرب
بدمید شمس ز ما غرب بد و ید الیه مهرولا
فوران نار ز ارض فا نوران نور ز شهرطا
ظهران روح ز شطرها ولقد علا و قد اعتلا
طیر العما تکفکفت ورق البهاء تصفصفت
دیك الضیاء تذورقت متجملا متجللا
ز ظهور آن شه آلهه زالست آن مه مالهه
شده آلهه همه والهه بتغنیات بلی بلی
بتموج آمده آن یمی که بکربلاش بخر می
متظهر است بهر دمی دو هزار وادی کربلا
ز کمان آن رخ پروله ز کمند آن مه ده دله
دو هزار فرقه و سلسله متفرقا متسلسلا

همه موسیان عمائیش همه عیسیان سمائیش
همه دلبران بقائیش متولها متزملا
بحر الوجود تموجت لعل الشهود تولجت
سفق الخمود تلجلجت بلقائه متجملا
هکل جمال ز طلعتش قلل جبال ز رفعتش
دول جلال ز سطوتش متخشعاً متزلزلا
دلم از دو زلف سیاه او ز فراق روی چو ماه او
بتراب مقدم راه او شده خون من متبلبلا
ز غم تو ای مه مهربان ز فراقت ای شه دلبران
شده روح هیکل جسمیان متخففا متخلخلا
تو و آن تشعشع روی خود تو و آن ملمع موی خود
که رسانیم تو بکوی خود متسرعا متعجلا

ایضاً

لمعات و جهك اشرقت و شعاع طلعتك اعتلا
ز چه رو الست بربکم نزنی بزن که بلی بلی
بجواب طبل الست تو ز ولا چو کوس بلی زدند

همه خیمه زد بدر دلم سپه غم وحشم بلا
من و عشق آن مه خو برو که چو زد صلای بلی بر او
بنشاط و قهقهه شد فرو که انا الشهید بکر بلا
چو شنید ناله مرگ من پی ساز من شد و برگ من
فمشی الی مهرولا و بکی علی مجلجلا
چه شود که آتش خیرتی ز نیم بقلهٔ طور دل
فسککته و دککته متدکدکا متزلزلا
پی خوان دعوت عشق او همه شب زخیل کرو بیان
رسد این صفیر مهیمنی که گروه غمزده الصلا
تو که فلس ماهی حیرتی چه زنی ز بحر وجود دم
بنشین چو طوطی و دمبدم بشنو خروش نهنگ لا

و من اشعارها الرشیقة قدس سرها

جذبات شوقك الجمت بسلا سل الغم و البلا
همه عاشقان شکسته دل که دهند جان بره ولا
اگر آن صنم زره ستم پی کشتن من بی گنه
فقد استقام بسیفه فلقد رضیت بما رضی

سحر آن نگار ستمگرم قدمی نهاد به بسترم
واذا رأیت جماله طلع الصباح کانما
ز چه چشم فتنه شعار او ز چه زلف غالیه بار او
شده نافه ئی بهمه ختن شده کافری بهمه ختا
تو که غافل از می و شاهدی پی مرد عابد و زاهدی
چه کنم که کافر و جاحدی ز خلوص نیت اصفیا
تو و ملك و جاه سکندری من ورسم و راه قلندری
اگر آن نکوست تو درخوری وگر این بد است مرا سزا
بمراد زلف معلقی پی اسب و زین مغرقی
همه عمر منکر مطلقی ز فقیر فارغ و بی نوا
بگذر ز منزل ماو من بگزین بملك فنا وطن
فاذا فعلت بمثل ذا ولقد بلغت بما تشا

و من غزلیاتها الجیده طاب رمسها

بدیار عشق تو مانده ام ز کسی ندیده عنایتی
بغریبیم نظری فکن تو که پادشاه ولایتی
گنهی بود مگر ای صنم که ز سر عشق تو دمبدم

اهجرتنی وقلتنی واخذتنی بجنایتی
بنموده طاقت و صبرطی بکشم فراق تو تا بکی
همه بند بند مرا چو نی بود از غم تو حکایتی
عجز العقول لدرکه نقص الحسوس لوصفه
بکمال تو که برد رهی نبود بجز تو نهایتی
چو صبا برت گذرآورد ز بلاکشان خبر آورد
رخ‌زرد و چشم تر آورد چه شود کنی تو عنایتی
قدمی نهی تو به بسترم سحری بناگهی از کرم
بهوای قرب تو بر پرم بد و بال و هم بجناحتی
برهانیم چه ازین مکان بکشانیم سوی لا مکان
گذرم ز جان جهانیان که تو جان و جانده خلقتی

و من ابیاتها اللطیفة روح الله روحها

جوانی چه آورد و پیری چه برد
بت خورد سال و می سالخورد
بت خورد سالیکه یك جلوه اش
ببرد از دل اندیشه خواب و خورد

می سال خوردیکه یك قطره اش
نخورد آنکه مرد و نمرد آنکه خورد

ز یك خم دهد ساقی روزگار
ترا صاف صاف و مرا درد درد

هزاران اسیر و بند و یکی
غبار علایق ز قلبش سترد

نه بازی است رفتن بمیدان عشق
که از صد هزاران یکی پافشرد

ز طوطی دعا دعوی از مدعی است
ببینیم تا گوی میدان که برد

ومن اشعارها المليحة عطرالله انفاسها

بعضی نظم ذیل را نیز از حضرت طاهره دانند و برخی نسبت آنرا بجناب نبیل «مورخ بهائی» دهند.

طلعات قدس بشارتی که جمال حق شده برملا
بزن ای صبا تو بساحتش بگروه غمزدگان صلا
هله ای طوایف منتظر ز عنایت شه مقتدر

مه مستتر شده مشتهر متـبـهـیا متـجـلـلا
شده طلعت صمدی عیان که بپا کند علم بیان
ز گمان و وهم جهانیان جبروت اقدسه اعتلا
بسریر عزت و فخر شان بنشسته آن شه بی نشان
بزد آن صلا ببلاکشان که گروه مدعی الولا
چو کسی طریق مرا رود کنمش ندا که خبر شود
که هرانکه عاشق من شود نرهد ز محنت و ابتلا
کسی ار نکرد اطاعتم نگرفت حبل ولایتم
کنمش بعید ز ساحتم دهمش بقهر بباد لا
صمدم ز عالم سر مدم احدم ز منبع لا حدم
پی اهل افئده آمدم هلـمـوا الی لـمـقـبـلا
قبسات نار مشیتی انا ذا الست بربکم
بگذر بساحت قدسیان بشنو صفیر بلی بلی
منم آن ظهور مهیمنی منم آن منیت بی منی
منم آن سفینهٔ ایمنی و لقد ظهرت مجلجلا
شجر مر قع جان منم ثمر عیان و نهان منم
ملك الملوك جهان منم ولی البیان وقد علا
شهدای طلعت نار من بدوید سوی دیار من
سر و جان کنید نثار من که منم شهنشه کر بلا

APPENDIX II

BAHÁ'U'LLÁH'S TRIBUTE TO THE BÁB AND HIS CHIEF DISCIPLES

Paragraphs from *The Kitáb-i-Íqán*

"THOUGH YOUNG and tender of age, and though the Cause He revealed was contrary to the desire of all the peoples of the earth, both high and low, rich and poor, exalted and abased, king and subject, yet He arose and steadfastly proclaimed it. All have known and heard this. He feared no one; He was regardless of consequences. Could such a thing be made manifest except through the power of a divine Revelation, and the potency of God's invincible Will? By the righteousness of God! Were any one to entertain so great a Revelation in his heart, the thought of such a declaration would alone confound him! Were the hearts of all men to be crowded into his heart, he would still hesitate to venture upon so awful an enterprise. He could achieve it only by the permission of God, only if the channel of his heart were to be linked with the Source of divine grace, and his soul be assured of the unfailing sustenance of the Almighty. To what, We wonder, do they ascribe so great a daring? Do they accuse Him of folly as they accused the Prophets of old? Or do they maintain that His motive was none other than leadership and the acquisition of earthly riches?

"'Gracious God! In His Book, which He hath entitled 'Qayyúmu'l-Asmá','—the first, the greatest and mightiest of all books—He prophesied His own martyrdom. In it is this passage: 'O Thou Remnant of God! I have sacrificed myself wholly for Thee; I have accepted curses for Thy sake; and have yearned for naught but martyrdom in the path of Thy love. Sufficient Witness unto me is God the Exalted, the Protector, the Ancient of Days!' . . .

"Could the Revealer of such utterance be regarded as walking any way but the way of God, and as having yearned for aught else except His good-pleasure? In this very verse there lieth concealed a breath of detachment, which if it were to be breathed full upon the world, all beings would renounce their lives, and sacrifice their souls. . . .

"And now consider how this Sadrih of the Riḍván of God hath, in the prime of youth, risen to proclaim the Cause of God. Behold what steadfastness that Beauty of God hath revealed. The whole world rose to hinder Him, yet it utterly failed. The more severe the persecutions they inflicted on that Sadrih of Blessedness, the more His fervor increased, and the brighter burned the flame of His love. All this is evident, and none disputeth its truth. Finally, He surrendered His soul, and winged His flight unto the realms above.

". . . No sooner had that eternal Beauty revealed Himself in Shíráz, in the year sixty [1260 A.H., 1844 A.D.] and rent asunder the veil of concealment, than the signs of the ascendancy, the might, the sovereignty, and power, emanating from that Essence of Essences and Sea of Seas, were manifest in every land. So much so, that from every city there appeared the signs, the evidences, the tokens, the testimonies of that Divine Luminary. How many were those pure and kindly hearts which faithfully reflected the light of that eternal Sun, and how manifold the emanations of knowledge from that Ocean of divine wisdom which encompassed all beings! In every city, all the divines and dignitaries rose to hinder and repress them, and girded up the loins of malice, of envy, and tyranny for their suppression. How great the number of those holy souls, those essences of justice, who, accused of tyranny, were put to death! And how many embodiments of purity, who showed forth naught but true knowledge and stainless deeds, suffered an agonizing death! Notwithstanding all this, each of these holy beings, up to his last moment, breathed the Name of God, and soared in the realm of submission and resignation. Such was the potency and transmuting influence which He exercised over them, that they ceased to cherish any desire but His will, and wedded their souls to His remembrance. . . .

"Do thou ponder these momentous happenings in thine heart, so that thou mayest apprehend the greatness of this Revelation, and perceive its stupendous glory."

—*The Kitáb-i-Íqán,* pp. 230-31.

APPENDIX III

THE WORLD RELIGION

A Summary of Its Aims, Teachings, and History

by

SHOGHI EFFENDI

Guardian of the Bahá'í Faith

THE REVELATION proclaimed by Bahá'u'lláh, His followers believe, is divine in origin, all-embracing in scope, broad in its outlook, scientific in its method, humanitarian in its principles and dynamic in the influence it exerts on the hearts and minds of men. The mission of the Founder of their Faith, they conceive it to be to proclaim that religious truth is not absolute but relative, that Divine Revelation is continuous and progressive, that the Founders of all past religions, though different in the non-essential aspects of their teachings, "abide in the same Tabernacle, soar in the same heaven, are seated upon the same throne, utter the same speech and proclaim the same Faith." His Cause, they have already demonstrated, stands identified with, and revolves around, the principle of the organic unity of mankind as representing the consummation of the whole process of human evolution. This final stage in this stupendous evolution, they assert, is not only necessary but inevitable, that it is gradually approaching, and that nothing short of the celestial potency with which a divinely ordained Message can claim to be endowed can succeed in establishing it.

The Bahá'í Faith recognizes the unity of God and of His Prophets, upholds the principle of an unfettered search after truth, condemns all forms of superstition and prejudice, teaches that the fundamental purpose of religion is to promote concord and harmony, that it must go hand-in-hand with science, and that it constitutes the sole and ultimate basis of a peaceful, an ordered and progressive society. It inculcates the principle of equal opportunity, rights and privileges for both sexes, advocates compulsory education, abolishes extremes of poverty and wealth, exalts work performed in the spirit of service to the rank of worship, recommends the adoption of an auxiliary international language, and provides the necessary agencies for the establishment and safeguarding of a permanent and universal peace.

Born about the middle of the nineteenth century in darkest Persia, assailed from its infancy by the forces of religious fanaticism, the Faith has, notwithstanding the martyrdom of its Forerunner, the repeated banishments of its Founder, the almost life-long imprisonment of its chief Promoter and the cruel death of no less than twenty thousand of its devoted followers, succeeded in diffusing quietly and steadily its spirit throughout both the East and West, has established itself in no fewer than forty countries of the world, and has recently obtained from the ecclesiastical and civil authorities in various lands written affirmations that recognize its independent religious status.

The Forerunner of the Faith was Mirza 'Alí-Muḥammad of S͟híráz, known as the Báb (The Gate) Who proclaimed on May 23, 1844, His twofold mission as an independent Manifestation of God and Herald of One greater than Himself, Who would inaugurate a new and unprecedented era in the religious history of mankind. On His early life, His sufferings, the heroism of His disciples, and the circumstances of His tragic martyrdom I need not dwell, as the record of His saintly life is minutely set forth in *The Dawn-Breakers: Nabíl's Narrative of the Early Days of the Bahá'í Faith.* Suffice it to say that at the early age of thirty-one the Báb was publicly martyred by a military firing squad at Tabríz, Persia, on July 9, 1850. On the evening of that same day His mangled body was removed from the courtyard of the barracks to the edge of the moat outside the gate of the city whence it was carried by His fervent disciples to Ṭihrán. There it remained concealed until such time as its transfer to the Holy Land was made possible. Faced by almost insuperable difficulties and facing the gravest dangers a band of His disciples, acting under the instructions of 'Abdu'l-Bahá, succeeded in transporting overland the casket containing His remains to Haifa. In 1909, 'Abdu'l-Bahá with his own hands and in the presence of the assembled representatives of various Bahá'í communities deposited those remains within the vault of the Mausoleum he himself had erected for the Báb. Ever since that time countless followers of the Bahá'í Faith have made the pilgrimage to this sacred spot, a spot which ever since 1921 has been further sanctified by the burial of 'Abdu'l-Bahá in an adjoining vault.

The Founder of the Faith was Bahá'u'lláh (Glory of God), Whose advent the Báb had foretold. He declared His mission in 1863 while an exile in Baghdád. He subsequently formulated the principles of that new and divine civilization which by His advent He claimed to have inaugurated. He too was bitterly opposed, was stripped of His property and rights, was exiled to 'Iráq, to Constantinople and Adrianople, and was eventually incarcerated in the penal colony of 'Akká where He passed away in 1892 in His seventy-fifth year. His remains are laid to rest in the Shrine at Bahjí, north of 'Akká.

The authorized Interpreter and Exemplar of Bahá'u'lláh's teachings was His eldest son 'Abdu'l-Bahá (Servant of Bahá) who was appointed by his Father as the Center to whom all Bahá'ís should turn for instruction and guidance. 'Abdu'l-Bahá ever since his childhood was the closest companion of his Father, and shared all His sorrows and sufferings. He remained a prisoner until 1908, when the old regime in Turkey was overthrown and all religious and political prisoners throughout the empire were liberated. After that he continued to make his home in Palestine but undertook extensive teaching tours in Egypt, Europe, and America, being ceaselessly engaged in explaining and exemplifying the principles of his Father's Faith and in inspiring and directing the activities of his friends and followers throughout the world. He passed away in 1921 in Haifa, Palestine, and, as already stated, was buried in a vault contiguous to that of the Báb on Mount Carmel.

According to the provisions of His Will, I, as His eldest grandson, have been appointed as First Guardian of the Bahá'í Faith and Head of the Universal House of Justice which must, in conjunction with me, coordinate and direct the affairs of the various Bahá'í communities in East and West in accordance with the principles enunciated by Bahá'u'lláh.

The period since 'Abdu'l-Bahá's passing has been characterized by the formation and consolidation of the Local and National Assemblies, the bedrock on which the edifice of the Universal House of Justice is to be erected. There are, according to the latest reports from Ṭihrán, over five hundred Local Assemblies already constituted in Persia. Organized Bahá'í communities are to be found in every continent of the globe. National Assemblies have already been formed and are functioning in the United States and Canada, in India and Burma, in Great Britain, in Germany, 'Iráq and Egypt.* Such Assemblies are in the process of formation in Persia, Caucasus, Turkestan, and Australia. Local Assemblies and groups have been already established in France, Switzerland and Italy, in the Scandinavian countries, in Austria and the Balkans, in Turkey, Syria, Albania, Abyssinia, China, Japan, Brazil and South Africa. Christians of various denominations, Muslims of both the Sunní and Shí'ih sects of Islám, Jews, Hindus, Sikhs, Zoroastrians and Buddhists, have eagerly embraced its truth, have recognized the divine origin and fundamental unity underlying the teachings of all the Founders of past religions, and have unreservedly identified themselves with both the spirit and form of its evolving institutions. All these centers function as the component parts of a single organism, of an entity the spiritual and administrative center of which lies enshrined in the twin cities of 'Akká and Haifa.

*Today there are over 120 National Spiritual Assemblies and more than twenty-five thousand Local Spiritual Assemblies around the world.

NOTES

1. Nabíl-i-A'ẓam (Muḥammad-i-Zarandí), *The Dawn-Breakers: Nabíl's Narrative of the Early Days of hte Bahá'í Revelation,* trans. and ed. Shoghi Effendi (Wilmette, Ill.: Bahá'í Publishing Committee, 1932).
2. Nabíl-i-A'ẓam, *Dawn-Breakers,* pp. xxiii–xxvi.—ED.
3. Tome 7, p. 474.
4. Nabíl-i-A'ẓam, *Dawn-Breakers,* p. 275.—ED.
5. According to *The Dawn-Breakers* Ṭáhirih was born in 1233 A.H. (1817–18 A.D.), the very year which witnessed the birth of Bahá'u'lláh. Thus she would be thirty-six years of age when she suffered martyrdom in Ṭihrán. [See Shoghi Effendi, *God Passes By* (Wilmette, Ill.: Bahá'í Publishing Committee, 1944), p. 73.—ED.]
6. ['Abdu'l-Bahá], *A Traveller's Narrative Written to Illustrate the Episode of the Báb,* trans. E. G. Browne (Cambridge: The University Press, 1891).—ED.
7. According to A. L. M. Nicolas, Ṭáhirih was born in 1753. See Nabíl-i-A'ẓam, *Dawn-Breakers,* p. 1, n.2.—ED.
8. According to *The Dawn-Breakers,* which has been published since I wrote this account in Iran in 1930, Shaykh Aḥmad passed on in 1827, at the age of eighty-one years, and is laid to rest in Medina.
9. Siyyid Káẓim, according to *The Dawn-Breakers,* was born in Rasht in the province of Gílán in 1793. He had memorized the Qur'án before he was twelve years old. In 1806 he lived in Ardibíl; later he went to find Shaykh Aḥmad and studied with the latter in Yazd; in 1817 both were together in Ṭihrán. Siyyid Káẓim went to Karbilá in 1822 and taught there until his passing on in 1843.
10. Nabíl-i-A'ẓam, *Dawn-Breakers,* p. 45.—ED.

11. Her father had bestowed on her the name of Umm-i Salmih, but she is never spoken of by this name.
12. Karbilá and Najaf are place of pilgrimage only for Shí'ih Muslims.—ED.
13. See 'Abdu'l-Bahá, *Memorials of the Faithful,* trans. Marzieh Gail (Wilmette, Ill.: Bahá'í Publishing Trust, 1971), pp. 175–90.—ED.
14. *Memorials of the Faithful* was published in English in 1971 by the Bahá'í Publishing Trust in Wilmette, Illinois.—ED.
15. Mírzá Ḥusayn of Hamadán, *The Taríkh-i-Jadíd,* trans. E. G. Browne (Cambridge: The University Press, 1893).—ED.
16. Nabíl-i-A'ẓam, *Dawn-Breakers,* pp. 81–82.
17. Dr. Luṭfu'lláh Hakím was elected a member of the Universal House of Justice, the Supreme Institution of the Bahá'í Faith, in 1963.—ED.
18. Nabíl-i-A'ẓam, *Dawn-Breakers,* p. 272, n. 1,2.—ED.
19. Nabíl-i-A'ẓam, *Dawn-Breakers,* p. 272, n. 3.—ED.
20. Ibid.—ED.
21. A covered carriage for travelers, placed on a mule or other animal.—ED.
22. Nabíl-i-A'ẓam, *Dawn-Breakers,* pp. 273–75.—ED.
23. The date of the murder was sometime between August 13–September 1847 A.D., as it was 1263 A.H.
24. Mosque.—ED.
25. Siyyid Asadu'lláh was a faithful believer, and his daughter was a sister-in-law of Ṭáhirih.
26. According to *The Dawn-Breakers,* Mírzá Hádí was the son of Mírzá 'Abdu'l-Vahháb-i Qazvíní (p. 80) and Mírzá 'Abdu'l-Vahháb was Ṭáhirih's own brother (p. 285).
27. Some historians say that Bahá'u'lláh Himself came with a large escort and brought her into the city. An excellent account of her journey to Ṭihrán is given in *The Dawn-Breakers,* pp. 283–87.
28. Both these young men, Riḍá Khán and Mírzá Ṣáliḥ, were martyred in 1849 when this fort was overcome.
29. The law of retaliation. —ED.

30. Nabíl-i-A'ẓam, *Dawn-Breakers,* p. 293.—Ed.
31. According to *The Dawn-Breakers* (pp. 347–39), Bahá'u'lláh visited Fort Ṭabarsí and His coming brought rapture and good counsel to Mullá Ḥusayn, the Bábu'l-Báb. It was Bahá'u'lláh who urged that Quddús be sought, for the latter was in captivity, and Bahá'u'lláh told them how Quddús could be freed.
32. In Baghdád in 1863.
33. The word kalántar means "mayor."
34. He was martyred in Ṭihrán, September 15, 1852. He was a merchant, a plain devoted Bábí, and he wrote a book about what he saw and heard from 1844 to 1852. He had promised to write more in detail about Ṭáhirih, but his martyrdom prevented this.
35. Qur'án, Sura 109 (Rodwell Translation).—Ed.
36. I read in one history that only at first was Ṭáhirih put into the little house outside, for the ladies of the kalántar's household loved her so much, they asked that she come and live in the home, and she had a room with a balcony on the second floor of the house. She must have been there for three years or more, and as the imprisonment was not too rigid, she did meet many people who came, under various' pretexts, to listen to her conversations.
37. The guards.—Ed.
38. Heretic.
39. The grandson of Ṭáhirih who lives in Ṭihrán told me in March 1930: "I heard from my own father that Naṣiri'd-Dín Sháh asked three important mullás to come and speak with Ṭáhirih. At this discussion they asked her, 'What are the proofs of your Faith?' From the Qur'án she proved it. The mullás tried their best to go against her, but they were not able to answer her. The shah wished a second discussion to be arranged, but in the second meeting the mullás did not permit Ṭáhirih to come. Rather, with great haste they begged the government to have her put to death. Náṣiri'd-Dín Sháh did not wish Ṭáhirih to be persecuted."

40. Retribution overtook this kalántar. Nine years later the shah, seeing one of his deeds, ordered an executioner to prepare ropes and twist them around the neck of Maḥmúd K͟hán and choke him instantly. He then ordered the kalántar's body to be hung on the gallows.
41. Nabíl-i-A'ẓam, *Dawn-Breakers,* pp. 621–29.—ED.
42. Quoted in Nabíl-i-A'ẓam, *Dawn-Breakers,* p. 629–30, n. 1.—ED.
43. Ibid.—ED.
44. Ibid.—ED.
45. Ibid.—ED.
46. Nabíl-i-A'ẓam, *The Dawn-Breakers,* pp. 667–68.—ED.